From George MacDonald's sermons...

"Do not be content not to grow. If you are not growing bigger you are growing less. If the light is not increasing the darkness is encroaching."

"The man that loves well, when the true time comes, will outstrip all the searchers in the knowledge of the very things that the intellect desires to understand."

"It is better to love a little than to understand everything."

"Every Christian ought to be a refuge. I believe that, if we were like Christ, even the wild beasts of our woods and fields would flee to us for refuge and deliverance: and man must be in the world as He was in the world, and then the world will blossom around him with all God's meanings, and not merely with men's sayings."

PROVING
THE
UNSEEN

George MacDonald

BALLANTINE BOOKS • NEW YORK

All rights reserved under International and Pan-American Copyright Conventions. Published in the United States of America by Ballantine Books, a division of Random House, Inc., New York, and simultaneously in Canada by Random House of Canada Limited, Toronto.

Library of Congress Catalog Card Number: 88-92837

ISBN 0-345-35369-2

Manufactured in the United States of America

First Ballantine Books/Epiphany Edition: May 1989

Contents

Prologue

I can scarcely think of anything more thrilling than discovering an old, neglected George MacDonald manuscript of some unpublished novel that time has forgotten. I have even dreamed of such a thing, much as I used to dream as a boy of finding an old cigar box full of rare gold coins in some musty attic.

William Petersen has made if not quite so sensational a discovery, surely an equally inspiring one, in locating a series of heretofore unpublished sermons by MacDonald.

During his long public career, in addition to writing some fifty-three published books, George MacDonald (1824–1905) lectured and preached countless times (no doubt many hundreds) to enthusiastic audiences and congregations throughout Britain and the United States. Today such spoken words would be preserved. But in the nineteenth century such talks were usually forgotten unless the speaker chose to record them later in book form. Tape recorders were still seventy-five years off.

During his tenure as editor/publisher of *Eternity* magazine, William Petersen became acquainted with a series of issues of the publication *The Christian World Pulpit*, of which his own magazine possessed nearly a complete set during the years 1870 to 1895. The magazine reproduced sermons by some of that period's most notable preachers. And in-

cluded in that overlooked treasury were some two
dozen sermons by Scotsman George MacDonald,
preached at various times and places about Britain.
The first of these were published a few years ago (in
slightly edited form) as *Getting to Know Jesus*, and
the remainder now come to the public for the first
time in this new volume, edited by William Petersen, *Proving the Unseen*.

In his lifetime MacDonald did publish five vol-
umes of actual sermons, three of which were entitled *Unspoken Sermons*. This new collection,
however, is quite distinctive from what MacDonald
wrote. While the subject matter, the approach, and
the theology of the contents of these sermons is un-
mistakably George MacDonald, their texture and
flow is new. They are more direct, simpler of style,
straightforward. They are, in short, "spoken" sermons, not written ones, and convey a real personal
feel into MacDonald's character. They reveal the
man MacDonald, speaking directly from his heart,
interacting with people actually before him, without the ideas making the additional editorial jour-
ney through his intellect. I was excited when
reading them, for I sensed "This is MacDonald the
preacher, the lecturer, the man who moved and in-
spired audiences." I had long been familiar with
MacDonald the writer; now this gave my awareness
of the man a new dimension.

I am very pleased to see this valuable addition to
the MacDonald corpus now brought to light, and
sincerely hope it increases awareness of the princi-
ples taught by this man of God. I recommend them
to you, not because they make good reading but because—as with everything MacDonald wrote and
spoke—they point toward truth and toward the Au-
thor of truth whom George MacDonald served.

—Michael Phillips

Introduction

Years ago, when I was still a teenager, I discovered a book entitled *Unspoken Sermons* by George MacDonald. I remember one Sunday afternoon when I sat down and read it from cover to cover.

A normal teenage boy does not customarily read sermons on a Sunday afternoon, and I was a normal teenage boy. Maybe I should have spent more time reading sermons, but I didn't.

However, these were not normal sermons, and George MacDonald was not a customary writer. And I could never forget one sermon especially, called "The New Name."

For years I thought I was the only one who knew about George MacDonald and his unusual insights. But then, as I began reading C. S. Lewis, I found that Lewis had "discovered" MacDonald long before I had. In fact, Lewis acknowledged, "I have never concealed the fact that I regarded him as my master; indeed I fancy I have never written a book in which I did not quote from him."

As an atheist at Oxford, Lewis admired the writing of MacDonald. He assumed that MacDonald was a good writer "in spite of being a Christian." "It was a pity," Lewis wrote, "that he had that bee in his bonnet about Christianity." But the nudge that MacDonald's writings gave Lewis started his movement toward Jesus Christ.

After his conversion, Lewis began reviving interest in the materials of George MacDonald until today almost all of MacDonald's works have been reprinted.

MacDonald himself was a bit of a maverick. Born in 1824 in the Scottish Highlands, he was raised in a solid, loving Christian home. He married the daughter of a London merchant and entered the ministry when he was twenty-six years old. Two years later, however, he was forced to resign because of some of his unorthodox views.

He left the pastorate but continued preaching and lecturing. Increasingly, he turned to writing. First he attempted poetry and fantasies, but then he felt he could reach a larger audience by writing novels, and soon he became known for his novels, children's stories, and short stories, as well.

With eleven children, MacDonald didn't always find it easy to put bread on the table, but in spite of problems with finances and his health, there was no bitterness. He rejoiced in the goodness of God.

He continued to be a student of Scripture and he continued to speak in churches in England and Scotland. One statement regarding Scripture characterizes MacDonald's biblical outlook: "I am always finding out meaning which I did not see before, and which I now cannot see perfectly—for, of course, till my heart is like Christ's great heart, I cannot fully know what He meant."

Years ago, as I read his *Unspoken Sermons*, I felt that same excitement of discovery coupled with a deep humility that my present understanding is still very imperfect.

As I said, most everything that MacDonald wrote a hundred years ago has now been brought back in print.

But recently in some musty old copies of a British publication, *The Christian World Pulpit*, I discovered a cache of MacDonald sermons. These were not "unspoken sermons"; indeed, they were spoken, preached at various churches in England and Scotland, and taken down verbatim as he preached them.

These "spoken sermons," therefore, though edited from the original publication, are not as smooth as his writings, but perhaps convey a little more of the heartbeat of this great man. In editing, I have tried to retain the flavor of the spoken sermon but have removed some of the repetition and extraneous material that would not be meaningful today.

May these "spoken sermons" affect you as profoundly as MacDonald's book of *Unspoken Sermons* affected me many years ago.

—William J. Petersen

I have never concealed the fact
that I regarded him as my master.

C. S. Lewis

1

Faith, the Proof of the Unseen

PREACHED AT BRIXTON CONGREGATIONAL
CHURCH, BRIXTON

> *Now faith is the substance of things hoped for,
> the evidence of things not seen.*
> —*Hebrews 11:1*

We have been talking about faith ever since the
Lord came. It is not exhausted yet; and God forbid
that I should think that I know yet what faith is;
although I know a little what it is. I think the
meaning of the text is this: Faith is the foundation,
the root, the underlying substance of hope.

If you have any hope, it comes from some faith in
you. Hope, you may say, is a bud upon the plant of
faith, a bud from the root of faith; the flower is joy
and peace.

But what is the meaning of "the evidence of
things not seen"? I cannot find any meaning in that

1

translation at all. But I believe the true meaning of the original is the most profound fact in human history. And the true meaning is this: Faith is the trial or the proving of things not seen.

Upon that turns the life of every person, especially in the present day. This thing of faith means the whole recognized relationship of man to God and his fellows; it means the right position of the human soul in regard to God's truth.

Now, whenever you begin to speak of anything true, divine, heavenly, or supernatural, you cannot speak of it at all without speaking about it wrongly in some measure. We have no words, we have no phrases, we have no possible combination of sentences that do more than represent fragmentarily the greatness of the things that belong to the very vital being of our nature.

Much, much foolish talk has been uttered about faith. They used to say that it was antithetically opposed to works. Never was there greater nonsense. They used to say that Paul taught faith and James taught works—that Paul had gone too far and that James had to write his epistle to set him right. But none of us will ever find either Paul or James wrong, nor was there the slightest difference between them.

On the contrary, I assert that faith is simply the greatest work that a person can do. Taking it in its simplest, original development, it is the highest effort of the whole human intellect, imagination and will in the highest direction. Never does human nature put forth such power with such effort and with such energy as when exercising faith in God. So I say that faith is the highest, and sometimes the most difficult, work that a person can have to do.

In today's society it seems as if it is more difficult to believe than ever before. Indeed many people feel as if there is less faith in the world than ever there was before. And when they look in their own hearts, they recognize a degree of doubt, difficulty, and fear that appalls themselves.

What?! Is the whole thing going to vanish like "the baseless fabric of a vision"? All this story of Christ, His life and death, and the conquests that were made in His name: Is it all going to evaporate; will we be left with a world as it was before He came? Rest assured that Christianity will never pass away. It is the foundation of truth and life to all generations.

But what about the difficulty of believing in this scientific age? It is natural that we should doubt, with such cries on all sides of us, and the intellect so much more awake than ever it was before, and indeed the conscience not more asleep than before; and with one on this side and one on that side crying out "I have reached, I have probed, but I have found no God."

Settle this with yourselves to begin with. Not all the intellect or metaphysics of the world could prove that there is no God, and not all the intellect in the world could prove that there is a God. If you could prove that there is a God, that would imply that you could go all around Him, and buttress up His being with your human arguments regarding His existence. As soon might a child on his mother's lap, looking up into her face, write a treatise on what a woman was and what a mother was.

But do not think that God is angry with you because you find it hard to believe. It is not so. That is not like God. God is all that you can honestly wish Him to be, and infinitely more. He is not angry with you for that. And He knows perfectly well what the scientific man calls truth—although you will observe that he is always constantly and everywhere changing his theories—that what the scientific man calls truth is simply an impossibility with regard to knowing God. And God knows it.

Your brain, the symbol of your intellect, cannot receive that kind of proof which you have when you read a proposition of Euclid. It commends itself to your mind and your understanding. You say, "So it is, and it cannot be otherwise." But there is no such proof in regard to the Mighty God. And therefore I say that if you doubt the existence of the living God, He is not angry with you for that.

But I ask you, "Have you been trying the things not seen? Have you been proving them?" This is what God puts in your hands. He says, "I tell you I am. You act upon that; for I know that your conscience moves you to it. You act upon that and you will find whether I am or not, and what I am."

Do you see? Faith in its true sense does not belong to the intellect alone, nor to the intellect first, but to the conscience and to the will. That man is a faithful man who says "I cannot prove that there is a God, but O God, if You hear me anywhere, help me to do Your will."

That is faith. Obedience is faith. It is doing that thing which you may only suppose to be the will of God. If you are wrong and do it because you think it is His will, He will set you right. Faith is the turning of the eye to the light; it is the sending of the feet into the path that is required; it is the putting of the hands to the task of doing the things which the conscience says ought to be done.

People Who Did Things

You will notice that throughout the eleventh chapter of Hebrews, the chapter from which this text is taken, you find a list of people who did things. Some of them were made kings, and some of them were struck down. But it was all for faith, and nothing but faith. These people felt a live truth welling up inside of them and they reacted according to that truth. Though the world itself was set against them, they walked right on in the name of God and met their fate.

Therefore, the practical thing is just this, that whatever our doubts or difficulties, we must do the thing we know in order to learn the thing we do not know. The Master said, "If you know these things, happy are you if you do them." It is the doing that is everything, and the doing is faith. There is no division between faith and works.

But perhaps you have been trying to serve God for

many years and perhaps you do not feel that you have made much of it. Maybe you are still troubled in your soul—not whether you are of God, but whether He is really listening to your cries. "Where is He?" you say. "If He would but speak to me. I have been crying to Him for years, and I have never seen a sign out of the great void. Oh, if He would only show Himself, if He would give me just the smallest sign that He actually exists and that He cares about me. Then I feel I could go on and on forever."

But, honestly, I do not think there is any sign that God could give you but what you would begin to doubt again. I do not believe there is any miracle He could work before your eyes even, that soon you would not begin to doubt, and be just as lost as before.

God will not give us little things to spoil our appetite for great things. God will never be content until we are one with Him as He is one with Christ. God will not give us signs and wonders and these inferior things, for God's common and usual way is far better than His miraculous way, as we call it. If all of life were miracle, we would make it all common. God's usual way of doing things is the best way. He will not give us signs of anything outside to give us confidence in Him. Nothing will serve God until our faith in Him is complete. It is by the vision in our souls, our own feeling and perception of what God is, that we are able to believe in Him.

When you see God as Christ saw Him, you will believe, and any glimmer of the truth in regard to our Lord's nature helps us to believe and enables us to go on. What the intellect does with Euclid, the whole mind, heart, intellect, imagination, conscience, and will does with regard to God when you see God and know Him. As you do His will, your faith grows.

But you ask, "What is the way to this?"

What is your first thought in the morning? Is it "God is life"? or is it "What am I going to do first today at my work?" Is it "God is very rich and I am His child and He will see to me"? or is it "How on earth shall I get through the problems lying ahead?"

Are you afraid? Are the cares of this world overwhelming you? Then your faith has plenty of room to grow. If you aren't trusting God to suppress your fears and to get rid of your worries, then I'm afraid you haven't grown at all. And if you've been trying to serve Christ for thirty or forty years, it has been a kind of service that He does not care much about, and it is no wonder you can't go on. Perhaps you have been very careful about reading your Bible and going to church, and doing this or that thing that you think belongs to religion, but have you been doing the thing Christ told you? If you do that, I do not care whatever else you do; you cannot be wrong then.

The beginner is troubled about whether there is a God or not; the older Christian believes in a God but does not trust Him. What is the difference? You may think it horrible for a person to doubt the existence of God, and yet you, though you say you believe in God, are afraid of the trouble, the poverty, the opinions of the world, and you are ambitious to be on your way! Do you not see that you too are doubting God?

I would almost prefer that you did not believe in God than say that you believe in Him and yet He is nothing to you. When you feel inclined to say hard things about your atheistic neighbor, remember that there may be a beam in your own eye even worse than the speck in his. Indeed, it is because our life does not shine that others have stood up and said "There is no light."

Let Your Light Shine

What you have to do is to let your light shine. I do not mean that you should be an example to other people. You have no business setting yourself up as an example; you have to be and to do, and that is letting the light shine. It ought not be possible to mistake a Christian for a person of the world. Your very dealings with others should demonstrate what Christ would have done for that man or woman.

If Christ were to come in upon you in the middle of your business day, would you be ready to turn to Him and say, "Master, this is how I am explaining things to my friend; this is how I see things in the light of Your love"? Would you be ready for that, or is most of your life conducted on a different level? If you conduct your life on laws other than Christian ones, you're altogether wrong. Christ is God, the all-in-all, or nothing at all. If every Christian were as the bush that burned with fire, atheism would soon vanish, unbelief would draw in its horns, and this sinful world would be condemned by the very presence of living faith.

Faith is the trying of the things unseen, the putting them to the test. Whatever your doubts or fears may be, try Him by obedience and then you will get help to carry on. Less than that won't do; other than that won't do. The darkness of life's closing time will come round about you and find you very doubtful, very sad, looking, looking into the darkness and wondering and worrying. But if you believe that the Son of God died and rose again, your whole future is full of the dawn of an eternal morning, coming up beyond the hills of this life, and full of such hope as the highest imagination for the poet has not a glimmer of yet. No one who has not faith can hope.

Faith is the trying of the thing that you do not see and that you cannot be sure about. Step out for God. He has given you a new opportunity. It will be the start of a fresh faith which you have not thought of before. Indeed, it will even give your life a new start. Faith is intended to put to the test the unseen world of truth, love, law, hope, and redemption. God grant that you will have faith enough to carry on from point to point until the faith shall vanish into light and until you never have to think about faith anymore, nor church, nor the Bible, nor prayer, but your entire being shall be a delighted consciousness of the presence of God and His Christ.

2

The Family of Jesus

PREACHED IN THE CONGREGATIONAL
CHAPEL, THE GROVE, SYDENHAM

*While He yet talked to the people, behold His
mother and His brethren stood without, desiring to speak with Him. Then one said unto
Him, Behold Thy mother and Thy brethren
stand without, desiring to speak with Thee.
But He answered and said unto him that told
Him, Who is My mother, and who are My
brethren? And He stretched forth His hand toward His disciples and said, Behold My mother
and My brethren. For whosoever shall do the
will of My father which is in heaven, the same
is My brother, and sister, and mother.*

—Matthew 12:46–50

A little sad, wasn't it, that His mother and His
brethren were not sitting about Him? For as an-

other evangelist says, "He looked round on those that were about Him."

His disciples were nearest to Him, and His mother and His brothers were outside. They did not know Him yet. It takes a long time and, what is more, a true heart, to know someone. There are people who belong to the same family through the whole of a long life and do not know each other to the very end.

Do you realize that His mother and His brothers had set out to stop him? That is why they were outside.

That lovely mother of His was not the first person to understand Him aright. Of course, she understood a great deal, and when the sword had gone through her soul, she would understand Him well. But there were other women, and they not so lovely as she, far less lovely in some ways, who understood Him better, because the sword had already passed through their soul, and they recognized the evil thing that had brought them to His feet.

But His mother and His brothers were outside desiring to speak to Him, because they said "He is beside Himself." He was going too far, and they felt they must stop Him. If His own family didn't tell Him that He was making a fool of Himself, who would? They felt it was a relative's responsibility to stop Him from playing the role of a madman.

Tens of thousands of so-called Christian people are doing the same thing in our present day, simply because they don't have any more of Christ in or about them than the common name that is given freely enough and is easy enough to carry. And there are tens of thousands more who are honest about being followers of Christ, but yet know so little of what was in Him or what He meant to do that they too would stop Him.

It is sad for anyone to be called by His name and yet not know Him.

If it is true that we are made in the image of God, then the paramount, absorbing business of our existence is to know that image of God in which we are made and to know it in the living Son of God, the one and only ideal Man. The older I grow, the more absolutely convinced I am of this; I have no words strong enough to put the statement in.

But alas, most of us like to pare away the words of Christ instead of looking at them until they fill heaven and earth.

Let us see what He meant by these lovely, precious, awful words.

"Who are My mother and My brethren?" He asked. And then He answered His own question, "Whoever does the will of My Father in heaven." You observe that He is always talking about His Father in heaven. You would think He knew nothing else. He has but one word, as it seems, over and over again. It has been said that He was possessed with love for humanity, and that is true; but He was possessed before that, and at the beginning of that, with love for His Father in heaven. That was the root, the power, the energy of all that was manifest even in the eternal Son of God Himself. It could not be otherwise. He was not to be misled with any outside shows of power and beauty. He knew the heart of them all, and this was the living will of God, by which all things arose, subsisted, and went on growing and growing. The Father was all-in-all in the heart of the Son, and because the Father, therefore the children.

Does it make you sad that He said these words to His disciples, that He does not seem to include the rest of the company and does not seem to include His mother and brothers? Is it a hard word?

Oh, the power of God Himself can give you nothing worth having but what the few about Him had already taken. They had already begun to partake of God's eternal life. Life is the only thing; it is the essential of well-being.

In the Act of Doing

We so often choose death, the thing that separates and kills. You see, everything that parts us from our fellow, and everything that parts us from God, is a killing of us. Whosoever is wide and free and will do the will of God—not simply understand it, not simply theorize about it, but do it—is a son of God. It is in the act of doing that man stands up as a son of God. He may be ever such a philosopher, ever such a theologian, ever such a patriot, ever such a philanthropist; but it is only he who in the act, in the doing of the thing, stands up before God, that is a son of God. This is the divine dignity: "My Father worketh hitherto, and I work." It is he who works that is a son of God. Do I mean outside works or inside works? I mean whatever a man does, whether it be the giving up all that he has to go and preach the gospel, or whether it be putting down the smallest rising thought of injustice, of anger and wrong, or of unselfishness in his soul.

The act is where the will of man stands up against his own liking, against temptation, and leads him simply to do that which God would have him to do, easy or difficult. It may be to mount a throne; it may be to be sawn asunder.

What is the man who does what God would have him do? "My brother," says Christ.

The woman who does that? "My sister," says Christ.

And as if He would go to the very depth of tenderness, He is not satisfied with saying "brother" or "sister"; He also says mother. Woman that has longed to have children and has none, did you ever think that you might have the Son of God for your son? If you would be the mother of the Son of God, do the will of His Father, and you will not mourn long.

But was He putting away His mother? Was it an unkind, unfilial thing to say? Did He in saying "Who is My mother, who is My brother?" repudiate the earthly mother and the earthly brother and sister?

Oh no, but it is a profound truth that our relation to God is infinitely nearer than any relation by nature. Our mother does not make us; we come forth from her, but we come from the very soul of God. We are nearer, unspeakably nearer, infinitely and unintelligibly nearer to God than to the best, loveliest, dearest mother on the face of the earth.

The Lord, first of all, spoke a profound truth when He said that, but then He goes deeper and deeper still.

If a mother has two children, one of whom is as bad as a boy can be, and the other as good, the one is her child and the other is not her child. They are both born of her body, but the one that loves her and obeys her is born of her soul, yea, of her very spirit; and she says, "This is my child," and she says to the other with groans, "You are none of mine." And his not being a son is the misery of the thing; she would die for the one that is no son to her.

So when we become the sons and daughters of God indeed by saying "Oh, my Father, I care for nothing but what Thou carest for; I will not lament for this thing, because I see Thou dost not care about it and I will not care either"; when you say, "This is sore to bear but it is Thy will and therefore I thank Thee for it, so sure am I of Thy will O my Father in heaven"; when we come to be able to talk like that, then we are in the same mind as Jesus Christ whose delight and whose only delight was to do the will of His Father in heaven.

But for God's sake don't cling to your own will. It

is not worth having; it is a poor, miserable, degrading thing to fall down and worship the inclination of your own heart, which may have come from any devil or from any accident of the birth or from the weather or from anything. Take the will of God, eternal, pure, strong, living, and true, the only good thing; take that and Christ will be your brother. If we knew the glory of that, I believe we could even delight in going against the poor small things that we should like in ourselves, delight even in thwarting ourselves.

The Importance of Family

Was Christ refusing His mother? Was He saying "I come of another breed, and I have nothing to do with you"? Was that the spirit of it? The Son of God forbid! Never, never. But I must show here a deeper and better thing. It is of the wisdom and tenderness of God that we come into the world as we do, that we form families, little centers, and groups of spiritual nerves and power in the world. I do not see how in any other way we come to understand God.

And oh! you parents who make it impossible for your children to understand God, what shall be said of or for you? If we had not fathers and mothers to love, I do not know how our hearts would understand God at all; I know not how I ever should. Then, again, if we had no brothers and sisters to love however should we begin to learn to know this

essential thing, that we should love our neighbor—
that is, every person that comes near us to be affected by us with look or word—as ourselves? It
were an impossibility. God begins with us graciously and easily; He brings us near first to
mother, then to father, then to sister, then to
brother, brings us so near to them that we cannot
escape them. The months of infancy and the years
of childhood are unspeakably precious from this
fact, that we cannot escape the holy influences of
family. So many are our needs, so quiescent are our
needs, that love is, as it were, heaped upon us and
forced into us; and we are taught, as we cannot help
learning, to love. But woe to the man or woman who
stops there, and can only love because the child or
the brother or the sister is his or hers. The same
human soul, the same hungry human heart, the
same aspiring, though blotted and spoiled, human
spirit is within every head, dwelling in every heart,
and we are brothers and sisters wherever God has
made man and woman. And until we have learned
that, we are only going on, it may be a little, to
learn Christ, but we have not learned Him.

What! Shall Christ love a man and I not love
him? Shall Christ say to a woman "My sister," and I
not bow before her? It is preposterous. But then my
own mother, my own father, my own brothers and
sisters—if they be His, too, they come first, they
come nearer. But I do assert that there is a closer,
infinitely closer relation between anyone that loves
God and any other that loves God than there is be-

tween any child and any mother where they do not
both love Him. The one has its root, the other has
its leaves and flowers, as well. We cannot love anybody too much; but we do not, we can never love our
own child aright until we have learned to love not
the mildness of the child but the humanity of the
child, the goodness, the thing that God meant that
came out of His will—that is the thing we have to
love even in our children, or else the love is a poor
dying thing, because we ourselves are dying.

If we love God, dearer and dearer grow the faces
of father and mother, wife and child, until there is
no end to it; it goes on not only eternally in time but
eternally in growth, expanding. Every bit we get
farther we understand more, and perceive more,
and feel more.

Are you lonely? Has lover or friend forsaken you?
Has Death taken father or mother, husband or wife,
sister or brother from you? If you could see aright,
that is a trifle, a profound trifle; for God's trifles are
precious and great. Dear in the eyes of God is the
death of His saints. But it is a trifle. He has abol-
ished death. He died, and He was not dead; up He
rose again radiant with light and victory. So are
they all who believe in Him; for "he that liveth and
believeth in Me shall never die." You may defy
death. Only have the patience of Christ; we have
that phrase—wait in His name, and you shall have
all you want. For when Christ has had His way
with you, then you have your way with Him; for He
says, "Ye shall ask what ye will, and it shall be

given to you." And when He has His way with you, you would as soon ask for anything that He did not like as you would beg of God to destroy the universe He had created. There would be nothing to you desirable that is not desirable in His eyes. Think of this, that you can have One who is more than brother or sister, father or mother, husband or wife or child—One from whose heart flowed out all these; One from whom came the love that analyzed itself into all these forms because of its infinitude. You can have Him for your own Friend, for Brother, Sister, Mother, Son. Whatever relation is possible in humanity, that relation does the heart of Christ feel to everyone that can take it.

Do you want, therefore, to forget and to take Christ as a make-up for the others that are gone? Never! Never! That is not His way. For how constantly does He tell you to love one another? That is the glory of Christ's teaching; that is His gospel; there is not an atom of selfishness in God or in Him who delights to see us loving one another. He cannot be satisfied except by seeing us love each other perfectly; that is His delight. Nay, more than this, I repeat, we cannot love one of our own aright unless Christ is in us making us love that person to the ideal of that relationship. Never father loved child, never child loved father, to the ideal of fatherhood and childhood, unless Christ was not only born in him but had grown up in him; and in none has he grown to that degree that he understands thoroughly, feels thoroughly, believes thoroughly, or anything like thoroughly, any relation of life so far as I know.

Do not be afraid to claim from Him what He gives you and would have you take. Claim Him as your own, for without Him you are nothing. Claim Him by taking the will of God for your one care, your one object, your one desire, and Christ will be yours altogether. "Behold I stand at the door and knock; if any man hear My voice I will open the door and I will come in unto him and sup with him"; partaking of the same food together, that food being the very will of God: "It is my meat and drink to do Thy will." That is the very food of which our Lord says "Man shall not live by bread alone but by every word that comes forth from God." The will of God is the very food and drink of the true heart; and when Jesus and the man who has opened the door to Him sit down together, it is to share together in the understanding of the will of the Father of both —that Father to whom He went when He said "Tell them I am going to My Father and your Father, to My God and your God."

3

Alone with God

*Stand in awe, and sin not: commune with your
own heart upon your bed, and be still.*
　　　　　　　　　　　　　　—Psalm 4:4

*Who shall ascend into the hill of the Lord? Or
who shall stand in His holy place? He that hath
clean hands and a pure heart; who hath not
lifted up his soul unto vanity, nor sworn deceitfully.*
　　　　　　　　　　　　　　—Psalm 24:3,4

It is a great sight to see a multitude of human
faces around you; but the whole thing I would
rather forget. Even when I stand before an assem-
bly to speak, I would much rather forget the gathering and meet the individuals gathered. I prefer

21

speaking to the single heart and soul of an individual; I have no ambition to move the masses.

The true power of life lies in the one soul. The whole gathered mass is but a heap of human sand except in proportion to what is awakened in the hearts of individuals. There is no religion, no praise, no worship, but of the individual. And then in proportion as the individual worships, there is something that rises from all the hearts and combines them into one before the face of their Father in heaven. But if the individuals do not know God, no gathering of multitudes brings them any nearer to the throne.

You see, my text is just what must be said to every single, solitary person. It addresses you in the most solitary, silent time—when your day's work is done and you are going to sleep.

In all the tumultuous going on of life, in all our eager pursuit, whether for pleasure or wealth or bare livelihood, we do not take much time to think seriously about God. But I tell you that if we make an end of anything else than the kingdom of God, we are of those who "lift up their souls unto vanity" and "who swear deceitfully."

The tumult of the day goes by, the pleasures of the evening pass, the last meal is taken, the good night is said. As if we were preparing for our grave we lay aside our work clothes and we lay ourselves out straight on our beds. There we lie, and God spreads the curtain of darkness around us, so that He may shut Himself in with His child.

It is God and His child then, or else God is left aside, shut out from His own child, and you are with something else than God.

Now the Psalmist David knew all about the storms of the world. For a man learns quite as much in going about the wilderness and fighting for his life as he does sitting behind a desk in a modern office. And when you have to protect yourself on all sides and carry out your schemes in the face of multitudes of enemies, you learn to know a great deal about man. And David, calm and solemn, would have understood us, perhaps better than we know ourselves. The word he would say to us, and I cannot think of a better word for us, is this: "Commune with your own heart upon your bed, and be still."

Silence in the Soul

Still! It is not bodily stillness alone. Little as we think of it, God has us in His hands far more than any mother has her little child of a week old. You cannot help going to sleep; He makes you. You do not know what sleep is, with all the philosophy you can bring to bear upon it; you, so busy all the day, when asleep are still, like death, and anybody might kill you. There you lie, passive, helpless, but not forgotten. If it were not for this sleep—that is, the bodily silence—we should all go mad. You know that sleeplessness is the first step to madness. If there never be a silence in the soul, and a man goes on always with his own thoughts and schemes and endeavors, it brings about a moral and spiritual madness. That is tenfold worse than mere madness of the brain, when a man judges everything by false ways, puts a wrong value upon everything, thinks little of great things and much of little things—that is a common way with all of us more or less, only, thank God, with some of us it is growing less.

There comes a silence every now and then; and God makes it just to put a stop to this kind of thing, and give Himself a chance of speaking. Do you not believe, or can you believe, that there is all about us, and in us, an infinite thought; that the atmosphere in which we live and breathe, as the fishes live and breathe in the sea, is thought, and that thought is the thought of One, and that One is the thought whence we came—that is the thinking God, thinking always? God's thoughts are power; they are like our thoughts, with this difference: They are self-made and ours are received from Him. You cannot tell a moment before it comes what thought you are going to think. You cannot think at all in a certain sense; your thoughts are only the shadows of God's thoughts; God is the living, original thought, and this is the atmosphere in which we poor little human creatures live. Poor do I say? To live in such an atmosphere, to live by it and to breathe it, and be unable to exist without it, and yet do I say we are poor? Ah! poor if we do not know it. Ah! poor indeed if we value it as little and think about it as little as the fishes that swim in the sea.

Friend, you are close to God, infinitely closer than your imagination can represent to you, and if you do not know it you are in the very essence a poor, foolish thing, whom God has not forgotten, though. But it is not in the midst of the tumult of life that a person first of all is able to hear God. We have not got up to Jesus Christ yet; God was always with Him; He was never alone. So He is with us; but then Jesus knew it and felt it. "I know that Thou hearest me always; I am not alone, for the Father is with me." Even He, when night came— and, I suppose, partly because there was not the retirement in the poor little houses that He wanted—went out into the great temple of God, the house of God—out to the mountains, that there might be nothing between Him and God. In His love to us He had consented to a kind of veil being drawn between Him and some of the aspects of God. When He took our human form the form was His own, but the kind of form was ours. Christ took His own shape when He took ours, but He did not need to be just made as we are. A kind of veil came between Him and God, which was something like another kind of faith—namely, shady human faith. I mean shady compared with what He had before. The Son always has faith in the Father. That is an immortal faith, but now He has human faith, as well; and, therefore, somehow it was better for Him to go out and be alone, with nothing between His heart and the heart of the Father, just that He might lie still and let God and Him be, and nothing else. The only name that will do for our God is "I am that I am." There is no describing it. "I am." And for us, when we are nearest God, it is just when we are in the knowledge that He *is*.

This is what David felt. When the tumult of his day was over he lay down in his bed, and then God was and David was; there was nothing else for the time. That is the fountain of life to which we have to go to draw life, just to be at peace and let God let us know that He is there; it is just to let all the rest go away, all the troubles and anxieties of life, and let God say to our hearts, "Here I am, and here you are; you are in My charge, and nothing can hurt you, everything is well; I am here in peace, and I am leading you through these dreams of the day-time with all those troubles and pains; I am leading you up to My eternal peace, no dull existence, but with a sense of joy such as I have in My own heart, such joy that compelled Me to create in you, such joy as you have in the sense that you are My child." Something like that it is between God and the man who knows how to be still. Let God speak to him. And this is what He wants to bring us to even by means of the tumult of life.

I think God sometimes has great trouble in separating us far enough from Himself that He can look round and know us. A mother will take her child and set it just as far as her arms can reach and draw back a little, so that the child may turn and run back to her. That is the first and most important lesson—the richest lesson that is given us in all our lives, just to run back to our mothers. And that is what God has been doing all the time through all the ages. I do not know how He has made me. I shall only say what trouble my Father had to get me just far enough from Him in order to let me know and choose Him. Then am I of His kind when I know Him, and choose Him, and go back to Him. This thing is what He wants us to know. Oh! let the work of the day tire us. When the work of the day does not tire us, and we keep going on with it, there is no peace when we go to sleep. We dream about rubbish, and we know nothing about God at all. But sometimes we lie down and think, "Oh, how stupid I have been; I have been forgetting my high calling, I have been fretful and distrustful, I have been unkind, I was not fair to that man, I have been cross to my own flesh and blood; it has not been a good shiny day with me." We think like that, and lift up our cry to the heart of our being, to the living, pure, loving Father, who cannot bear to see a spot on His child and who has patience for a thousand years to get rid of that spot.

Fathers Like Windows

Ah! that is a Father, indeed. The best of fathers are but little windows compared with God; and some fathers are very smoky windows, and have made a very wavy distorting glass for the child

through him to see the path to eternal life. If we cry
to Him so, then sometimes there comes down upon
us a peace, a rest, and an awareness of what He is
and what we are. We get strength and hope, we may
even be able to sleep; and often because we cannot
get it any other way, or cannot get enough of it any
other way, He gets us ill and sends us to bed. This is
just another way to bring about that peace, that
quiet of heart in which God can speak. It seems
then the most natural thing that God and man
should thus meet, and know, and understand each
other, that there should be the meeting together of
the thought of the one with the thought of the other.
That is the simplest, most reasonable, common way
and, therefore, I would say to some who doubt
whether it can be God that is speaking to them, because it seems to come in such a natural way just
out of their own hearts—I would say to them, "God
is so near you that He cannot speak into the deepest
of you, and you become conscious of it without its
coming through the most reasonable, natural chan-
nel; for all that you do not know of your own being
joins on to what you do not know about God's." Our
best thoughts come to us just simply in our souls
like our bad ones, only they come from a much
deeper source. Bad ones are not half so deep as good
ones, and it seems "Can this be? Am I not thinking
this myself?" Yes, you are thinking it yourself, because God has thought it before you. And then you
do think it yourself, for there is no possibility of
dividing you from God. God thinks you out of Him-

self, and you live because He lives. God has set us to choose the right thing and do the right thing, and then we are willing, willing from ourselves, but those selves are of His making. They are not only rooted in Him, but their very existence springs out of His existence, and so we live and cannot be parted from Him. We are the heirs of Him, our Father; we are the heirs of eternal life, and partakers of the Divine nature, as soon as ever we give in to the real natural law of things, and say "Thou art my Father. I am doing Thy will." And this is all that Jesus wants of us. But we are so hard to bring to this that I say He makes us ill, sends us to bed, and we have to lie still, and, perhaps, we are not able to think much, only able to feel, and so He makes it quiet around about us.

Upon others, He brings sudden poverty. There comes a great shock, and then a silence, and then the person begins to think "What have I been about? If I were to fill myself with this money that I have been seeking, if it filled every pocket, and every box at my banker's, where should I have been? Without life, without hope, a hollow, empty, miserable thing, sending my God-born being out to inhabit the forms of sovereigns and banknotes, descending from my calling into this worship of the miserable."

Oh, friends, commune with your own hearts, with your own body, and be still, and know that there is a Power that made you, made your money, too, and does not care much about it. It is not a sign of God's favor to give much money to people, and most heartily do I not only believe because Christ said it, but because I see that it is hard for a rich man to enter into the kingdom of heaven, and I find it hard enough, being a poor man. It is not easy, but it is worth doing. It may not be easy to banish from your soul the things of the day that you may be still and hear God; but oh, is God worth nothing? Is the presence closer than that of husband, or wife, or child, or brother? Is the presence of this loving Power that loves you out and out, is it nothing to you? Do you prefer to write so many figures as your possession to having God yourself? It is awful folly, and yet you and I are always in danger of it, and every time we are miserable about what may happen tomorrow, we are denying God and saying He is not enough for us. It is just as you have seen an ungracious child or an ungracious beggar sometimes snatch your gift from you. You see an ungracious dog do it sometimes, but not often. If you loved God His gift to you would be a living gift, and you would use it for Him. Reaping and keeping to oneself is altogether against the heart and thought, the very being of God, who lives in giving, from whom there is always a going out, and out, and out.

If we do not do the will of God in the day, it is not likely that we will be still upon our beds that He may come and visit us. We need not be without Him during the day. Though not a businessman myself, I sympathize with you who have so many things to think about. A thousand things pressing upon you,

it must be so difficult for you to remember God, and
I know it is such poverty, such wretchedness, not to
remember Him. But if you commune with your
hearts on your bed, and are still, and God comes to
you there, there will come a moment, even in the
midst of your business, when a quiet will drop down
upon you like a little bit of heaven covering your
head, as it were, for a moment, and you think, "Oh,
there is God, and if God is there, how well all this
is!" Only what an awful thing, then, if you do not,
from that thought, go up like a very priest of God in
His temple dispensing righteousness in truth—I do
not mean in talking; I do not mean speaking about
the Bible, but I mean in buying and selling, and in
common speech, and in the common things of the
day, for there is nothing in this world to be done
that is not honorable in itself, and may not be, and
ought not to be, a service—a service in the temple
of the living God. It is indeed serving God if a man
can make his counter the very altar of the living
God; the goods he puts down upon it are holy before
God, because they are placed there in honor and in
service. I believe that the true temple and the true
worship is an every-day-of-the-week worship. That
is what our Lord would have. You do not hear Him
talk what we commonly call religious talk. He did
not talk the religious talk of His day, but when He
does talk, it is as deep as the foundations of the
universe; it is God and man, and that is real religion. It is not this observation and that observation;
it is my soul and His soul, and then my hands to do

His will; that is real religion. It is the deed that
stirs the man; it is the thing you do, and not what
you feel.

One man lamented to me that sometimes it
seemed to him as if he had no feelings at all; that he
inherited from his poor father who had no feelings,
or next to none; but his hands and his heart were
busy for his fellow creatures from morning to night,
and his prayer ascended to the God of his salvation.
We were not meant to be creatures of feeling; we
were meant to be creatures of conscience toward
God, a sense of His presence; and if we go on, the
feeling will come all right. Our feelings will blossom as a rose just from the very necessity of things.
And blessed is the man whose highest, deepest feelings come to him when he is alone on his bed and
still.

But if even that man does not go out, and carry
with him the principle that God is all-in-all, he will
be the worse. Let us be careful, above all things, if
God has given any insight into the reality of His
Being, and our relation to Him, and let us be tenfold careful about our fellow man, that we do him
no wrong.

"Who shall ascend into the hill of the Lord? He
that hath clean hands and a pure heart." Some of us
lead homely lives and have not the temptations
that others have. We have our own temptations. It
is so easy to be rough in the house, so easy to lay
aside our good manners to our spouses and children.
Who shall know the eternal Father, and come forth

and not be a gentle one? God will be readier to come to His child the next night if during the day he has been living childlike, walking in the steps of his Father, holding fast by Him. If he has been good to his fellow children, to his brothers and sisters, wherever they are, God will be readier to meet him, readier to say "My child, here I am." The one eternal, original, infinite blessing of the human soul is when in stillness the Father comes and says, "My child, I am here."

4

The Only Freedom

Paul, a servant of Jesus Christ
—*Romans 1:1*

In addressing the Romans, Paul seems to identify himself as "a servant of Jesus Christ." But it is more than that, that he says.

The translation should be "Paul, a slave of Jesus Christ."

Again, when Paul is writing to the Philippians, he joins Timothy with him and says, "Paul and Timothy, slaves of Jesus Christ."

You see, the word means more than "servants." It is certainly not what we would call a servant in our day, for servants in Roman times could not come and go as they pleased. They were not even servants who had been taken in war and thus had become slaves; the word means more than a bond-slave. It means a born slave, and there we have it—"a born slave of Jesus Christ."

Though it is a figure of speech, it does not mean that it is less meaningful to us. Where there is a figure used in the New Testament, it means more than it can say; and more than any word that man can utter did Paul mean when he said that he was a born slave of Jesus Christ.

No doubt, there is in the word an element that Paul did not mean and did not feel. You know how a mother will sometimes, just out of tenderness to her child, call it a bad name. So Paul here, just in the despair of faith, takes delight in belonging to Christ utterly, altogether, inconceivably, saved by Christ Himself, for he could not tell or feel how much he belonged to Christ. And he used a word that indicates in it something that was not real, not true. Although he says "I am a slave of Jesus Christ," yet if any man in this world was free—besides the Lord Himself—that man was Paul. So Paul did not mean to imply that there was not freedom in Christ.

"But," you say, "Paul was an enthusiast."

Yes, I agree that he was an enthusiast; and if he had not been an enthusiast about such a thing as this, he would not have been worthy to be a slave to the lowest of Christ's people. There is no reality in the relation of things that are high if we be not enthusiastic about them, if they do not possess us, hold us, fill us, lead us, drive us, teach us, feed us, live in us, and make us live in them. No good can be done without enthusiasm. There is no reality of love without enthusiasm.

What! Shall I know anything at all that is genuine about Jesus Christ? Am I a fool capable of believing that man came from the bosom of the Father to be to me my loving Brother and my Savior; to take me, at His own torture, out of my misery, out of myself, which is my torture, into the life of His Father in heaven? Shall I believe that—shall I even believe that He had not a selfish thought in Him, and not be enthusiastic about Him? Have I the faculty of enthusiasm in me? Is it possible for me to give myself away—to do anything that is not urged and suggested by the lower self? Am I capable of these things at all? Then, if I am not enthusiastic about Jesus Christ, this whole faculty of my nature lies useless, rotting in me, for there is nothing else in the universe to call it out, or capable of calling it out. The poor enthusiasms that one sees in the world for things that are less than the truth, or that are small passing facts of our condition here— look how they last when a man is vigorous and how they wither when he grows older. But you will find that Paul, at the very last of his life, was more a slave of Jesus Christ than ever he was—far more His slave than when he lay struck blind and helpless by the light of His appearing.

For my part, it seems to me a grand proof that a man like Paul, brought up as he was, with such a brain and such a heart, should be capable of burning with such enthusiasm for a man of whose history he knew very little that was real or true until he saw Him in heavenly glory—that after that he should live to be the rejoicing slave of Jesus Christ —is it a wonder that such a fact should weigh with me ten times more than the denial of the highest intellect of this world, who talks as if he understands my faith, but knows nothing about it? Paul knew the Lord Christ; and, therefore, heart and soul, mind, body, and brain, he belonged to Jesus Christ, even as His born slave.

A Slavery Which Is Liberty

But let us try to understand a little what is meant by a slavery which is a liberty. One of the first feelings of youth is a love of liberty. In our history a boy has been taught it from his earliest thought, and he feels that the grand thing is that he shall be free and the slave of no man. As a rule he has a very low notion of what liberty is, and in most cases it does not grow very much better as he gets older; but still there is, at the root of it, something genuine and real, which is capable of being interpreted into a high and holy thing. What is it, as the boy thinks about it? Well, it is just to do as he likes; or, if he carries it a little higher and thinks of political liberty, it is that nobody may meddle with him, that he is to stand without any weight, or bond, or command upon him. And for the sake of this kind of liberty, too often he will bind his soul in chains of misery. Sometimes, for instance, he will run away from school; he will shirk doing the things that his parents tell him; he will run away from home; and, in order that his feet may be free to wander where they will, he ties up his inner man in a sense of wrath, in garments of pain, in a feeling of bondage; and because he would be free he makes himself a slave far deeper than any outward law could make him.

Suppose, however, that there was no law of parent, or teacher, or magistrate, or ruler of any kind laid upon us, and suppose that the man has plenty of money and all kinds of what he calls freedom to go and do what he pleases. Suppose that, outside, he is aware of no bondage whatever. That cannot last long. As soon as there comes a touch of pain, the least sense of weakness—as soon as the first white begins to come on the hair—well, perhaps not quite so soon as that, but when he has the first feeling "I am not quite capable of what I used to do"—as soon as any of these merest touches come on the consciousness of a man, the sense of freedom begins to go. But suppose that in the heyday of a man's strength, in the heartiness of ripe youth, before middle age has begun to come, he can move as he pleases and do as he wills, and suppose that there is no one to say nay to him, is he free? Is he free?

Would you say "For this end came I into the world, that I might do whatever I liked"? And would you feel that you were grand and free? If you do feel so, you are a most wretched slave, for your very ideal is slavery; your every high notion is mean and despicable. You cannot see it; I know that, but you do not see everything yet; and the time is coming when you will be compelled to see it, and can no more help seeing it than now you can help—or, rather, I should say, will help not seeing it. For what is it that drives you on? There is a devil who has whispered to you—affected, perhaps, a certain convolution of your brain, touched you at some certain spot; and you say that you are free, and all the time you are the real sport of a temptation. You call it liberty. You stay till the point of the arrow that directs you turns against you and pierces you to the center. You stay till the devil that tempted you mocks you, and you gaze at him and get no help, for there is no such thing in the world as liberty, except under the law of liberty; that is the acting according to the essential laws of our own being—not our feelings, which go and come.

The man that will rage one hour and be cold the next—what a fool he is if he supposes that he is to walk either by his rage or by his coldness. It is a law that he is to obey. He is to follow the lines upon which this being of his is constructed, this central, original, heart-emotion of his existence. Why, as soon might a man attempt to drive some great engine backward—as soon might he lay hold of its center pinion and try to stop it, as you can think to make it go well with your being if you live contrary to the very essence of your being; for, let me tell you, you are not bad, or, if you are bad, you are damnably bad. You are not made bad. God forbid! For God made us, and He made nothing bad, and if you will be bad that is fearful indeed. The lines of our being are laid, I will not even say by the hand of the living God, they were laid in His heart. The idea of every one of us was known and thought over in that heart; and, out of His heart we have gone. He has set before us a way that we may turn and, of our own free will, run back to Him, embrace the Father's knees, and be lifted to the Father's heart.

There is no liberty but in doing right. There is no freedom but in living out of the depths of our nature—not out of the surface. You lose your temper. You think that you are free when you go into a rage. Half an hour after you are ashamed; and yet you think that you are a free man. You acted out of the mere surface of your nature—something which it needed but half an hour to make you ashamed of. That is not liberty. That is acting out of your poor, mean, despicable self, and not out of the divine self, the deepest in us, for the deepest in us is God.

We did not come into this world because we willed it. We did not say what we should be. It is God in every man that enables that man even to stretch out his hand. The moment may come when he can lift it no more. Let him will, and will to do it with an agony of willing; yet he cannot raise his hand any more. He cannot do it. It is God; none else.

Liberty in Obedience

This is the thought that I want to impress upon you: The only true liberty lies in obedience. Can you comprehend that?

Do you think that Jesus Christ would have felt free one moment if He had not been absolutely devoted to the will of His Father in heaven? Suppose it had been possible for Jesus Christ to have been less devoted to His Father. Do you think that He would have felt that He was a free man?

Do you not think that that was what made the devil? He had a notion of being free: "Here I am. I will be the slave of no one—not even of the God that made me." And so evil enters the universe and all goes wrong, and he is the devil, not an archangel any longer, and a mean devil at that, a devil who tries to pull all down in the same abyss with himself, well knowing that he cannot even give them his pride to uphold them.

Well, then, we are the born slaves of Jesus Christ, but then He is liberty Himself, and all His desire is that we should be such noble, true, and right creatures that we never can possibly do or think a thing that shall bind even a thread round our spirits and make us feel as if we were tied anywhere. He wants us to be free—not as the winds— not to be free as the man who owns no law, but to be free by having God's law in our hearts and by being incarnations of God's truth. When you know that the law goes in one way, is it freedom to bring your will against that law, or to avoid it and to go another way, when the very essence of your existence means that you do not oppose but yield to the conditions of your being, those conditions that make your being divine, for God has made us after His own fashion?

When we do as God would do, when we act according to the divine mind and nature, we are acting according to our own deepest self, which is the will and law of God.

But let me show you a little more. I do not say that the moment you begin to obey the Lord Jesus Christ and to be His slave, that then you know what is meant by liberty.

Many things we know are right, but we are not inclined to do them. Other things we know are wrong, and we are inclined to do them. But when the law of liberty comes, the will of Jesus Christ, we begin to try to do the things we are not inclined to do and not to do the things that we are inclined to do.

Fighting for Freedom

But do you not see that here is a strife? So long as we are in this condition, as long as we know that we have to do the things that we do not like and that we must not do the things we would like, we are not free. We are only fighting for freedom, but we are not free. We do not know liberty yet; and yet, on the other hand, if we like the good thing and did not like the bad thing and, without any thought or effort of our own, just went to the good thing and not to the bad thing, we should not be free either, because we should be going just by the impulse in us. So there comes a contradiction which it is not easy to explain or understand. But, you know, God could not be satisfied to make us like the animals.

A good dog does not bite because he is not inclined to bite. He loves you, but you do not say that he is high morally because he is not inclined to do anything bad. But if we, choosing, against our liking, to do the right, go on so until we are enabled by doing it to see into the very loveliness and essence of the right, and know it to be altogether beautiful, and then at last never think of doing evil, but delight with our whole souls in doing the will of God, why then, do you not see, we combine the two, and we are free indeed, because we are acting like God out of the essence of our nature, knowing good and evil, and choosing the good with our whole hearts and delighting in it.

It is not enough to love because we cannot help it. We must love, too, because we will it with our whole nature, and then, do you not see, when we come to love one another perfectly, we do not need to be told "Thou shalt not steal; thou shalt not kill; thou shalt not bear false witness," because the thing is absolutely abhorrent to us, if the thought would come up at all. But when we have learned to love our neighbor as ourselves, the thought of killing and stealing never comes out, or of defrauding or of doing ignoble things and calling them "business." Nothing of that kind. We positively love our neighbor, and to hurt him would be to hurt ourselves worse. That is liberty, but we can come to that only by willing it, the root of our being is that will. We must fall in with it. We must will it ourselves, and then, at last, the lovely will of God will possess us from head to feet and fingers, and we shall live in the very breath of God and act like God Himself, free like the Living One, because we are one with the source of our life and our being.

So you see how we have got to deal with something like contradictions, but in the meaning of the thing your own heart tells you what it is, and you will see that there is no contradiction in it at all. Though it might be exceedingly difficult to lay it out all plain in logical language, your hearts can understand it. They witness to it because they have grown hungry. You want to be such children of God as this. You want to be free from oppression of evil in every way. The time will come when you will lay down the arms of your battle, fighting for the truth. You will have to lay them down even because you have conquered. How conquered? Because you are perfectly satisfied with God, one with His will, rejoicing in His joy, living in His life, having no fear, no ambition, no anxiety, but a constant strength of life that death and hell cannot touch. You would not be afraid then if you were cast into the middle of hell fire. The flames could not touch you. If you had a body that they could scorch and burn, yet the soul within you would rise superior even to that torture, because, being of the very nature of God, partakers of the divine nature, you would be able to bear pain in triumph and with a sense of freedom in the midst of it, and slavery would be far from you.

But I have a word to say to those specially who have belonged to Christ for many years. Can you say it out of your heart and mean it, "I am the slave of Christ?" Object to the term, and I say, are you the free man of Christ? For they mean the same thing. His slave is His free brother. Is there anything that you do now? We cannot divide our lives, we cannot say that the private gentleman will be saved when the man of business will be condemned; we are either all Christ's, or not at all, for He has told us that no man can serve two masters. Are you doing anything now that is not just all that you would like? Suppose the thing were to come to be laid open to the purest eyes of those who know you. If there is such a thing as you would not like seen, does the Master see it or does He not? If He does not, He is no Master: We want a greater. If you think He will let it slip, God forbid that I should serve that Master. I want a Master that will not pass over a farthing, a Master who will not let me go from His cleansing hand even if that hand be washing me with fire so long as there is any spot of defilement on my spirit; and the least shadow of dishonesty is the deepest defilement.

Are you not sometimes content with saying "I do

as my neighbor would do to me"? You cannot say "I do as I would like my neighbor to do to me," perhaps. I wonder whether you could say, then, what the Lord said, for remember He never said "Thou shalt love thy neighbor as thyself." That was not what He taught. That was taught long before. The Spirit of God taught it, but not by Jesus Christ. What Christ taught was "Love one another as I have loved you." Do we behave to our fellow men as Christ has behaved to us? If we do not we are not His slaves. We may be even following in the track of His triumph—I do not say that we shall not get in, but I am clear upon this—that we never shall enter until we have passed through what ordeal is needful to make us clean as God Himself. We have got to be good, and if we will not willingly to ourselves, He will make us. It is what He made us for, and it ought to be the business of our lives.

I will tell you what it is like. Suppose, for a moment, there is the Conqueror of all time driving in His chariot through the streets of the city. Amongst the enemy whom He has conquered, He has found children of His own, and He has said to those children, "Come up and ride with Me in My chariot"; and they say, "No; we will not." But He cannot afford to lose His children, and He will not lose His children. Therefore, they are tied to the chariot and dragged along with ropes through the streets because they will not mount and ride with their conquering Father, and that is just the condition of thousands and thousands of so-called Christians.

They are not free, and God will not let them go. They are tied to His chariot wheels, because of themselves they will not be children and ride hanging about the necks of their Father as He drives His conquering steeds.

5

Duty—Nothing

Which of you, having a servant plowing or feeding cattle, will say unto him by-and-by, when he is come from the field, Go and sit down to meat? And will not rather say unto him, Make ready wherewith I may sup, and gird thyself and serve me, till I have eaten and drunken, and afterward thou shalt eat and drink? Doth he thank that servant because he did the things that were commanded him? I trow not. So likewise ye, when ye shall have done all these things which are commanded you, say, We are unprofitable servants; we have done that which was our duty to do.

—Luke 17:7-10

If you love the Lord, you want to understand Him; if you take no trouble to understand Him, I do not think your love can be very great. And if you do not do what He tells you, He Himself will refuse you.

He does not want your acknowledgment of His dignity; He does not care for it; it is nothing to Him. If all the world bowed its knee to Him and did not understand or love its Father, He would not care one atom for it. "Why say ye unto Me, Lord, Lord, and do not do the things I say unto you?"

Let us look at something He says and see if we can understand it, and above all, let us see that we do it.

First of all, what He says in this passage is a parable. It is something to tell you how to act, how to do, how to think. If you put it to any use except a practical one, you will never understand it to all eternity. Parables are stories, tales, incidents, it matters not, by which we are to measure the action of our lives. You need not dwell on a servant plowing and the master's speech except for the sake of understanding what it means for you.

Of course, we cannot compare the customs of the East with ours, or allow the folly to enter into our minds that it was rather hard measure for a man who had been plowing all day to come and wait on his master when he came home. It was the order of things that a man should wait upon his master when he came home. And after the master had had his dinner, then the servant had his.

The Lord's object is made plain in what He says afterward. Do you not think that you are very fine people when you have done everything that is commanded you?

And yet, isn't that exactly what we do? Are not we ready, when we have done some poor little duty, to think that we are very fine people indeed?

But the Lord said, "Having done all that is commanded you, say, We are unprofitable servants."

Are you going to be conceited because you do not pick pockets? Perhaps you have some friends who occasionally pick pockets. Are you going to boast "I never did such a thing; I am a fine fellow; I am an honest man"? How ridiculous!

It just comes down to this—if we did nothing that was wrong whatever, we would have nothing at all to boast of.

Only Doing Your Duty

This is the only place where our Lord uses the word "duty." In the Authorized Version you will not find "duty" at any other time coming from the Lord's mouth.

Do you think that He came to teach us our duty? No, He did not. Let me say it again: When we have done all our duty, we are still unprofitable servants.

I believe the day will come when the word "duty" will be forgotten except as a matter of history, when the heart will be so filled with love to do the right thing, not because it is a duty laid upon us to do it, but because it is what it is—the loveliness of God shining through us—that we shall never think of its being our duty, but we will make haste with our whole nature to do it with gladness and song.

Don't be foolish enough to say that I imply for one moment that duty is not to be done! That is the devil's lie. There is no way of learning the glory of truth but by doing it even when you find that the nature of you is not good enough to love it utterly, and when you are tempted by that which is in you not to do it. We must begin to obey if ever we can hope to understand the glory of the truth. If a man comes to me talking about duty, or about any theory of religion, or the mind of God, I feel that I do not care to talk about these things except it be for the sake of a right order of action, for I hold that a man's opinion may be just as correct as it is possible for metaphysics and morals to make it, and yet he is no better, but rather the worse for it. It is not what a man holds with the intellect, but what he gives himself to heart and life and soul. It is utter mockery to God and man to talk about faith as distinguished from works, to talk about faith as if that consisted of holding this or that fact, or holding all the facts together when the man's soul does not give itself to the will of the Father. If we do not do the thing that the Lord Jesus Christ tells us, we are not merely unprofitable servants, we are lost souls, and God only knows what that means.

I do not understand how to trim the matter; I

only believe what the Lord tells me, and nothing else. And if He says: "Seek ye first the kingdom of God and His righteousness," then I know what I have got to do—I have to seek that God shall rule in me, and that I have and possess as my own the righteousness of God—that is, that I be righteous as God is righteous. I have to seek that, and any excuse that you can make about the demands of society, or the necessities of the world, or the need to look after what you shall eat and drink, or what you shall wear, or still less what kind of houses you shall have, or what horses you shall have, to countervail or run in the face of the Master, is simply preposterous in the place where we are supposed to meet and worship God in the name of Christ.

You see, the Lord gives us the loftiest possible standard. Now, I know what you are thinking. You say: "You are preaching perfection"; and then you begin to ask: "Do you think that is attainable in this life?" What care I to answer such a question as that? What is it to me? I know what I have to do is to strive after that which the Lord tells me, whether I be perfect here or there; I have nothing to say, and do not care to say anything. The energy and force of every man's nature—that is, if he is true as a Christian man, if he is the thing he professes to be—is to do as the Master tells him, and strive to be perfect, even as his Father in heaven is perfect. You see He gives us a high standard of perfection. Do all your duty, everything possible, and then think nothing of it; forget it. We are poor creatures,

we are unprofitable servants, we have only done
what it was our duty to do.

"Oh," but you say, "it is so hard!" Perhaps the
more you try you will find it the harder, and yet be
the less willing to let it go; the more you try the
more you will see that nothing less is worthy of a
man's energy; and the more you do the will of God
the more ready will you be to say "I am an unprofitable servant," for you will see the glory of God
looming up above you higher and higher, and feel
the hand of God under you lifting you up at the
same time toward His own height.

The Master Who Serves His Servants

Now let me take you to another passage of Scripture. It is also in the Gospel of Luke and it is also a
parable. Like the first story, it is also about a master and his servants.

> Let your loins be girded about, and your lights
> burning; and ye yourselves like unto men that
> wait for their lord, when he will return from the
> wedding; that when he cometh and knocketh,
> they may open unto him immediately. Blessed
> are those servants whom the Lord when he
> cometh shall find watching; verily I say unto
> you, that he shall gird himself, and make them
> to sit down to meat, and will come forth and
> serve them.
>
> —Luke 12:35–37

In the verses just before this story, Jesus has told His follower: "Do not make much of yourself; have done with yourself and your own ideas of your own glory. I will look after you; be My children, My servants, My good, blessed ones; never trouble yourselves how you stand in relation to other people; never let a thought of comparison cross your minds as to which of you is the highest; have done with that, and I will serve you; sit down at My feast." And here He says, "I will feed you when I have come home from the wedding."

These parables so often rise from the lower to the higher, so often even from the false to the true. Jesus will compare Himself even to the wicked, sometimes, that He may have the argument *a fortiori*. "Hear what the unjust judge saith," Jesus said in one parable. "And shall not God avenge His own elect?"

And so here He comes home. When He went home, it was not for a wedding. You know what He had gone there for—how tired He was; and even then He would have girded Himself as He did in the depth of His sorrow before He went to the cross, and would gird Himself and make them sit down to meat, and would come forth and serve them.

Was it because they had all done their duty and had become great men and conquerors?

No, not at all. It was because they were of His mind, because they were men that loved the truth, because they were men who loved good, who had cast away self and thought nothing of it. Though they were weak and frail, they were of His mind. So they shall sit down at His table and He will go and serve them, passing round and round, and giving them everything that they wanted.

Jesus Christ is not proud; God is not proud. Jesus Christ is not selfish; God is not selfish. He is perfectly clear in His devotion to us to deliver us from this mean self, this self-seeking. Oh, we have got so much of it we do not see it! I dare to say that every one of those who are feeling the least selfish now have got that in them which, when they come to see it, they will loathe. We ought to be sharp on ourselves, awake and alive to discover the evil thing—that which the Lord does not like. To those that will give up self I say He will be a tender, ministering friend, sister, brother, mother. Anything that you can put to represent help from one human being to another is what God will give, and does give, if we only let Him. "Whosoever will do the will of My Father which is in heaven, the same is my mother and sister and brother."

Now I think you will be able to put these two passages together, and see that although at first sight they may appear to contradict each other, they do not at all. If a truth is a great one, we cannot see it at all without seeming contradictions. If our brains are not fit for these big things, still less is our language and our logic fit for them. It is only the childlike spirit that can see it. The wise and the prudent look over the top of it. They do not get at it; they are busy with this and that; and all the time the child in its heart is crying out for hunger.

There is one thing only that we are quite sure about in this world, that we have no doubt about—that our time will come to pass away; and I say it is mere common sense that we should give a thought as to the possibility of what is beyond. For any man to say that that is not practical is to stamp himself a fool. Why, I know I have got my duty to do in this world, and we have just been learning here that we must do it, and think nothing of it. I know that, but I know also that doing or not doing my duty, the hour is at hand when all this life will just be crushed up into the smallest space.

Therefore it is a matter of mere common prudence, knowing you have to pass into an unknown region, until you can prove to your souls that there is no life beyond the grave, and until you can be sure that your proof is correct, and until nothing comes to make you doubt whether your argument be absolutely certain, you had better do something about the matter.

I say here is the report that a Man came who said: "I know God, and if you will listen to Me you shall be the sons of God; and if you will hear what I tell you, and do as I tell you, you shall have the power to be the sons of God." And when you look at what He tells you, instead of finding it is something mysterious, some strange form of things that you have to go through, you find that it is, in the parts you understand of it, the simplest, noblest, grandest thing that He requires of you.

Is it unpractical to try to verify this? If there were but the smallest whisper come to us across the ages, it would be the part of a wise man to say to himself "Well, this sounds strange, but if this Man, who, according to all reports was the best of men, tells me this thing, I had better try, whether it is true or not, and begin to do the things He tells me, in order that, as He says, I may know whether He speaks the truth, for He says, "If any man is willing to do the will of God, he shall know of the doctrine whether I speak of Myself, or whether I come from Him."

If you are made in the same fashion as I am, you will find that it is just the highest condition of soul and heart and mind to love that Man and His Father. I say to you, even if you do not love Him now, it is prudent of you, it is practical of you, to take the word that the Man says, and say: "If a Man like that could lie, whom am I to trust? Can I trust myself if a Man like that could lie about the greatest things possible to lie about? No, He must be right; at least I will try to find out if He is right, and if He is right then God hears the prayer that is offered to Him." Offered to Him! What do I mean by that? I do not like that phrase. God hears the prayers that I ask of Him, and, therefore, I will cry out into the infinite silence to see whether there be a God that will hear and answer me!

And if a man will not put the matter to that test, I have no more to say to him; I must leave him to God—shall I say till the Great Shepherd sends out some of His terrible sheepdogs after him, and then he may be glad to turn, when he can see or think of no refuge but the very bosom of the Good Shepherd Himself.

6

Knowing the Risen Lord

PREACHED AT HANOVER CHAPEL, PECKHAM

*Jesus saith unto her, Touch me not; for I am not
yet ascended to my Father: but go to my brethren,
and say unto them, I ascend unto my Father, and
your Father: and to my God and your God.*
—John 20:17

The Lord was dead, they said. His body lay in the
grave, and all that those who loved Him could do
was to try to make the Lord's cast-off garments last
a little longer—lying unseen, useless—nay, more,
slowly returning to the dust, but still to be kept a
little longer on the way. A poor consolation, and yet
it was all that they had left.

Mary Magdalene sought Him and found the place
empty. Well, there were angels, but even angels are
nothing if we have not seen the Lord. Peter and

John had come, but soon they, too, had left.

Mary Magdalene, however, could not leave the place. It was no wonder. Miserable because her Master had died and yet not believing in the risen Lord, she stayed by the grave. It is the same today. Many poor Christians stay by a grave, miserable because their friend has died, but not believing aright in the power of the resurrection.

While she was weeping, she saw the angels. They said to her, "Woman, why weepest thou?" They knew that there was no cause for her tears. None whatsoever. It was as if they had said "Those tears are not necessary."

And she answered: "Because they have taken away my Lord, and I know not where they have laid Him." She gave a reason for her tears; it was not that her Lord had died, but it was a misery on top of that, a superadded grief—the body was gone. Grief upon grief she bore.

She thought it a misfortune that the body of Jesus was taken away.

A misfortune? That word should never be heard from a Christian's mouth.

Why Was the Body Not There?

But why was His body not there? It was because He wanted His body for Himself. She was calling it a misfortune, but He was alive and in His body— changed though it was.

Often the very things that lift us up nearer to God are viewed by us as misfortunes. "How sad," we say, and we console one another on the means that the Father of our spirits is using to cleanse our souls, to take away the meanness, the poverty, and the nakedness of our souls, and to make us the very children of His heart.

When she spoke, she turned away from the angels. She did not care to look at them. They were beautiful, radiant creatures, but what were they to her—to a heart that wanted Christ? If Christ was dead and banished, what were live angels to her? She turned her back upon them. And then she saw Jesus standing there, and she did not know Him.

Why? Well, in this case you might say that she was weeping so much that she could not look at her consolation, just as the Lord was troubled that He could not get Martha and Mary consoled. I tell you that the Greek definition means when it says that Jesus groaned in His Spirit and was troubled, that there was displeasure in it, a gentle, loving dissatisfaction with them, that they would not take the comfort that He brought them. He told them that their brother should rise again. They did not heed, but wept on because their hearts were so sore. They were actually unwilling to receive comfort from the very source from which Lazarus, their brother, had been himself sent into the world to be their brother. The Lord was troubled and displeased. They were not right-hearted to Him for the moment. They thought, perhaps, that He might have done a little better if He had been there to keep their brother with them. Oh, it is lovely to see, though, that loving Jesus did not make them love their brother less.

The tendency of all true love is to expand, to throw wide the doors, and to say: "Come in, come in!" and one of the glories to me in my deep conviction of the eternity and infinitude of the Lord is that His heart is big enough just to be Jesus Christ to every single individual of us. Our hearts, you know, get a little bewildered with the number of people that they have got to love. We need eternity to go on learning to love, but Jesus is eternity unto every single creature in the world. He can come, and will come, close to them and recognize brother, sister, mother.

"He will give every one that overcometh a new name, a stone with a new name on it, that nobody knows but Him and me." That is what He says. There is a name for every one that the Lord knows. He knows what He wants to give you—a something that is a secret between Him and you, because only He can know your deepest individuality, and not the one best loved in the world can come near to know really what that name is—the name that tells what you are—what God meant you to be when He thought about you first.

To every one the sound will come close and nigh. And if He came to Mary thus, oh, thank God that He came to her first! She was no apostle—a woman who loved Him and whom He had set free from seven devils, whatever that may mean. He came to her first, the type of the whole rescued world.

But why did she not know Him? I have spoken to you of His eternity, His infinitude. All forms of humanity belonged to Jesus Christ. He can take any shape because it is His own. It is no changing. If you could know Him in one shape, you would know Him in every shape. If you could know Him in one, you would know Him in all. And it is very notable that He was not known by the two that went to Emmaus either, and that they were in doubt about Him also when He appeared on the seashore in Galilee. I think He took another shape that they might learn that He was the same Spirit, and that it would take all humanity to reveal Him. We must love like Him, love God perfectly, love our fellows perfectly, and then the Lord might take all our faces one after the other, and they would all do to reveal Him a little bit; but it would need them all together and infinitely more to reveal the eternity of His being.

The Gardener and His Garden

It may be that, perhaps, that made Mary not know Him at first. She thought He was the gardener. He was not shining now. Observe, He does not always shine; He keeps in His glory for our sakes. To help us somehow He keeps in His glory. The Lord will not give us too much at once. She takes Him for the gardener He is, and a lovely gar-

den He tends! Why, all the faces of the flowers reveal Him if you understand them. There is nothing
in the whole universe that we can call lovely, that
moves our heart or soul, but it is just a little shim-
mer of the heart of Christ. The flowers grow out of
His heart, as it were. But I fear you may not enter
into this. He is all revelation; He is all the atone-
ment; He is all the oneness.

She thought Him the gardener, and she said to
Him, "Sir, if thou hast borne Him hence, tell me
where thou hast laid Him, and I will take Him
away." And she would have done it, too. She was not
very strong after going through such days with her
Lord as she had gone through lately, but she would
have carried Him away somehow, you may be sure
of that, if she could have got that body. "Tell me
where thou hast laid Him" she said, humbly, to the
gardener, as she supposed; for this was a private
garden where He was buried. The tomb belonged to
Joseph.

Jesus would not keep her long. It was time that
the terrible cloud that was over her should be blown
away by the winds of heaven, and that the real facts
of things should show themselves—namely, the
eternal gladness of God. The well-being of the universe must come forth in her soul, and so He just
said to her one word. And what other word could be
so much to any of us as to be called by our name
from His lips?

If you have no notion of such a delight, if it
wakes in you no sense of radiance and of hope, I say

you are half dead; you are not alive yet; you are just in the condition in which Paul regards those to whom he cries "Awake, thou that sleepest, and arise from the dead, and Christ will give thee light." He just called her by her name, that is all. That is all that we want. When God called first He called "Adam." And now the Lord calls "Mary." What you call your "Christian names" will have a real meaning then, when you are such that the Master can call you even by them; only He has got a more Christian name yet—that one of which I have spoken—ready for you when you are ready for it.

But to be called by our name, the name that God has in the heart for us, or even by His lips, to be called by our own name—what is it? Do you not see that it acknowledges that you and He have got to do with each other? And so it is. If you are thousands of years from knowing it, that heart of yours has to do with the very heart of Jesus, everything to do with it. Oh, make haste and obey Him that He may call you by your name, knowing that you will answer "Master."

Do you know anything about Him, or is He only a phantom to you? You have heard about Him from your childhood. He seems a faraway mystery—a shadowy and solemn personage, and you do not know that He is your own brother—more your brother than any one that was born of the same mother could possibly be—infinitely more, and that you have got to mind your great Brother—the eter-

nal Brother who has come to take you back to His
Father.

Now this is just a picture of the redemption of
Jesus Christ. He has come to look for the children
that His Father wants—the little ones. He wants
them all about Him—all about His knees, in His
arms, nestling in His very heart—not merely in the
folds of His great garment, but in His very heart.
And so did the Father want us that He sent us His
own Son, to let us do what we pleased to Him, and
hurt Him terribly, and kill Him, that we might
know Him and go back with Him, after all the
wrong that we have done Him.

"Mary." "Master." You call Him "Master." Do you
do what He tells you? He is no master of yours if
you do not. You mock Him to His face, and He will
say "I do not know you." If you obey not the Lord,
you are none of His.

Call a man your master and not heed him? Do
you suppose that he is fooling when he tells you this
or that, and that you may do as you like about it, or
never open the paper with his instructions to see
how you are to pass the time, and how you are to do
the things that He has given you to do in this
world? You mock the living God. Oh! it is time that
those who call themselves Christians should know
that they are none of His if they care not for His
commands. If we did the thing that He told us, window after window would open in our soul till heaven
itself would surround us in every quarter. "Master!"

And then we seem to know from another part

that Mary fell down and laid hold of His feet. I do not think that any of the others did. Mary was the one to whom He appeared first, and she held Him by the feet; and then He spoke words that must have set you thinking—"Touch me not." Well, if you think it means anything unkind, anything repellent to the heart or soul or person of Mary, you are wrong. It did not mean that.

"Touch me not." Well, I think it means, according to the Greek, "Do not keep firm hold on me: Do not keep on touching me." It is not exactly "Do not detain me," but rather "Let me go." Just note why, though: "For I am not yet ascended unto the Father." Observe, it is not "I am not going just yet and you shall see Me again." I do not think that that is it. I think it means rather "Do not keep me now. I have got to go to my Father. I want to go to Him first."

The Secret of the Story

The secret of the whole story of humanity is the love between the Father and the Son. That is at the root of it all. Upon the love between the Son and the Father hangs the whole universe. What it can mean exactly, you know, I cannot tell you. Why the Lord must go and ascend to His Father, though with Him all the time and with Him at the moment, I cannot tell you; but it means something, as if there were some center somewhere where this very body of His must be embraced by the arms of the Father before

He was satisfied—as if He had to go back and tell His Father "I have done it, Father, I have done it. It is over now and we shall have them all back by and by."

Just observe that Jesus stops Mary's transport. It might have killed her perhaps with emotion, but He stops it by telling her to go and do something. He sends her. It is so blessed to be with Him, but the brethren do not know yet. They are lost in sorrow and lamentation still, and Mary, you are happy, but you must not keep it to yourself. "Go and tell them. I must not be detained. Let Me go (as it were), for I am not yet ascended to the Father. I have to go there first. But go unto My brethren." Observe that His message to the brethren is not to say "I have come back," but "I am going." He wants them to see that the main point is not that they are going to see Him again, although they are; the main point is that He is going to the Father. Now, you know that in all His life in the world it was always "My Father. My Father sends Me. My Father wants Me to do this, and to do that, and I do it. I am just doing what He tells Me, and now I am going back to Him."

But note the words now. You will see what is written. "Say to them" (this is the first message, remember, that the Lord speaks when He rises from the dead triumphant) "I ascend unto My Father and your Father, and My God and your God." If you could see into that you would shudder at the notion of doing a wrong thing again; and if you would see into it, for the sake of all divine illumination, do the thing that you know already, or you will not get more. That is the one way. Do not think that anything does not matter that you know to be right to do, and that you ought to do, and then you will come to know and to understand.

"I ascend unto My Father and your Father." What? Are we all one? Are we one family—Christ, and God, and us? That is what He means. Whether you can receive it, whether you can care for it or not, it is the one thing that God and His Son care for. "I in them and Thou in Me, that they all may be one in us." All the care of the heart of God is unity. "Give Me My children, and let us be one," He says to His great eternal Son; and so the Son sends the message: "Go and tell My brethren." Oh, yes! it looks like something theological when it says "brethren"; but it just means brother, of course. It is only the old word. It is just as good—"Tell my brothers." And He gives the message to a sister, mind you. A woman is the first messenger from the risen Lord to men. "Go and tell My brothers that I am going up to My Father and your Father."

Of the Same Breed

We have got the same Father as Jesus Christ has. We are of the same breed. And the shame—oh, the shame, the ugliness of the thing, when we act of the devil and not of our Father!—yea, not to men-tion the devil, when we act from our own mean, paltry, as-yet unredeemed selves—our poverty-stricken ideas of ourselves. Why, the notion that the proud man or the proud woman has of him- or herself in their highest moments of exaltation is a contempt beside the knowledge of what we are in the idea of God, and what we have to become—poor, miserable creatures, able to be proud of themselves, for it is the deepest degradation possible that a man should be able to be proud and satisfied with his own poverty-stricken nature, for which he has constantly to give mean, paltry excuses in order to keep himself on the least degree of good terms with himself. And yet Jesus says "My Father and your Father."

I say that because we are born of God and refuse to be the sons and daughters of God, the shame that lies upon us is of the deepest and blackest, just a thing that if you could see it you would loathe and say "What a beast I am." David felt something of it, or whoever wrote that psalm, "I was as a beast before thee"; and when Job gets a sight of God, in some way which we do not understand, but suppose that it was just a revelation to his soul of the splendor of God—when he gets that there is no more arguing. He is down before God, and he abhorred himself in dust and ashes. His whole nature he feels to be so poor and wretched before the loveliness, the truth, the grandeur of the living God.

O friends, believe that Jesus Christ knew what He was talking about. You may find it difficult, just because you have a poor idea of Jesus Christ, although you call Him so good. It is quite possible for men to say "Oh, God is so grand and great," and to put all the fine adjectives to His name possible, and yet their notion of Him is of something not fit to be a God. It is quite possible. Oh, learn Him as He took such pains to show us what He was; learn Him as He was.

I am wrong. I should not say "was." There is no "was" with Him. He is the same. Just what He appeared on the earth He is now, and is in the earth still. Oh, I wonder which of us would know Him if He came now. Could we discover anything in the shape? He reproaches them that they do not know Him. He says: "You never knew God. You never saw Him. You never heard His voice, or you would know Him." We ought to know something of God. We ought to have heard enough of God to know Christ as He came to us. "Well, but," you say, "I am not sure that I should know Him." Well, I grant you I am afraid that I should not, either. I do not know, but I am sure of this—that I never shall know Him if I do not obey Him. I am sure of that. And if you want to know Him, so that He cannot escape you, and you would find Him anywhere, wherever He was, in the midst of a crowd or on the hilltop, do what He tells you, and He will go on helping you on and on, till at last you shall see His very self.

"And tell them that I am going up to God, to my Father and your Father." We do not know Him as Christ did. God is more His Father in that way, because Christ knows all about His Father, and we are poor little children, and cannot know what our great Brother knows. Oh, we may know Him with the whole of our nature, for we need Him as much, and no more or less, in that way, than Jesus Christ did.

The whole of the universe was nothing to Jesus without His Father. The day will come when the whole universe will be nothing to us without the Father, but with the Father an endless glory of delight. Observe that the Lord is "My Father and your Father." But He is not quite content with that, and remember that He never speaks unnecessary words. He says, "And to My God and your God." Because, after all that the word "father" could teach those of us who have had the very best of fathers, "God" means more and more, and better and better, for ever and ever, than even that best of words signifies to me. "My God and your God," for God is more than a father in the same direction—further and further in the same direction. It is as if the Father could but take you to His bosom, but God takes you inside Him, into His very soul. If you have lower thoughts of God than these, it is pitiful, and you do God no honor, and you do yourself much wrong.

7

To the Church of the Laodiceans

PREACHED AT THE CONGREGATIONAL CHURCH, WIMBLEDON

And unto the angel of the church of the Laodiceans write: These things saith the Amen, the faithful and true witness, the beginning of the creation of God.

—Revelation 3:14

It was natural that the Lord should appear to the Apostle John, the friend whom He loved so dearly. It was also natural that He should use him to give a message to all of us whom He would make His friends.

He might appear to any one of us if we were fit to see Him or if it were good for us to behold Him. But I fear that many of us, if He did appear, would not know Him. Some of us would even turn our backs on Him. He would not fit our preconceptions of Him at all.

No, I do not suppose any of us are fit to see Him, nor do I think that it would do us good. But He sends us messages, such as this message through the Apostle John. And we know that whatever He has said once, He means now, for He is unchangeable.

Now I want you to consider this message that He sends in the third chapter of the Revelation. It is His message to the last of the seven churches. But I want you to notice first of all that every one of the letters to the seven churches comes to the church as a collection of individuals, and every one of the messages ends with an appeal to the individual. And unless your company is composed of individuals who love God and His Christ, it is no church at all—lest the organization of it be perfect, it is no church at all. Every one of them ends with "He that hath ears to hear, let him hear what the Spirit saith to the churches." The churches will never be better, the world will never be better, but as the individual is better; and if any of you would help the world to be better, the first, the best, the prime essential thing is to be better yourself. That is the way to better the world. What, will you go and teach a man to be good when you might be better and do not care! The individual is the constant appeal of the Lord Christ, and this is just like Him; all the messages here are just like what we have read in the story of Him in the world. He seems constantly to be trying to rouse the individual perception of truth, the individual sense of duty.

You must note that in this last message to the Laodiceans, He has not a word of praise for them— not a word of praise. Almost all the rest have some praise given them, but there is not a word of praise for these halfhearted Laodiceans. They want to go comfortably on, and not to be troubled much, and they will get into heaven as they please, in some sleepy way or other. They won't find themselves comfortable there. It is not the halfhearted, simmering kind of hearts that the kingdom of God and His Christ is for. Had God been halfhearted you would never have had a chance of life eternal. It is because God is true-hearted, unselfish, out and out devoted to His creatures that there is any world at all.

And He won't have you as you are! If you correspond at all to this description of those that made up the church of the Laodiceans, God won't have you— you won't do! What a word of indignation this is!

Oh! you are quite wrong if you have the fancy that Jesus Christ is one who is always speaking soft words. He is indignant sometimes, He is angry sometimes, but there is not one atom in that indignation, in that anger that is not love. But His love will not make His blow lighter, and you are afraid of that kind of love because it demands so much. It demands that you shall be fit to come into His very arms, to His very heart, and less than that will not do. It cannot be that He shall embrace evil things;

He will have us free, cost what it may; if it takes an eternity to clean us, we must be clean.

Neither Cold Nor Hot

What a word almost of contempt! Only there is no contempt in Him. Using our language it sounds like it, but I call it "indignation," and the strong effort of His heart of love to make them feel what a low condition they are in. "Neither cold nor hot—I won't have you; I will spew you out of my mouth." That Christ should speak like that to us and we deserve it—who will endure it? But, oh! it is of the mercy of God that He speaks to us like that.

How is it that we can be spoken to like that? Because we are made after His image. If we were not made in His image He would not speak to us thus. Oh, it is a mark and a sign, true as heaven, that we are of God's kind, and therefore deserve to be spoken to so because we are not of His kind. I speak by a contradiction, but it is right. You are His children; why will you not be His sons and His daughters? He, the Father of us, to be driven to use such words to us because we love darkness more than light!

He speaks very plainly what He thinks of them, and He shows very clearly how His thought about them ran counter altogether to their own judgment of themselves. "Oh, we are all right! We accept this and that doctrine; we believe so-and-so; we are all right." Or, on the other hand: "We have broken free from the traditions of the elders; we have got a better way, and so we are all right." Are you doing the things that Jesus Christ tells you? If not, you are all wrong. Your ideas, your opinions, your systems, let them be as correct as astronomy, and you are no better, but probably much the worse for them. The simple heart that just goes to do the thing for Jesus for love's sake, or the thing that his Father makes him feel is the right, noble, God-like thing—that is the man whom the Lord will acknowledge and confess before the Father.

It is terrible to think how we shroud the Son of God in a cloud of our foolish, low, paltry ideas about Him. We have swathed Him in the doctrines of the Church and the traditions of men, and the Lord Christ, the Brother-man, we scarcely see. The individual heart does not turn to Him as to its very goal of thought, and feeling, and judgment, and hope. You think you are rich and have need of nothing. All right, you do not know that you are wretched, miserable, and poor, and blind, and naked. Does the Lord say this for the sake of abuse or for the sake of telling us we are that? No; He wants to rouse us—"I counsel thee"—He wants to rouse us up, to open our treasure houses that He may fill them, to open doors and windows that the breath of God may blow through our souls. That is why He says the hard words, but hard words in the right places are the kindest thing.

Immediately after He has spoken these terrible words He says, "As many as I love I rebuke and chasten." That is what accounts for all the trouble in the world; and He will "rebuke and chasten" until the man gives in. But just note. I said to you there was not a word in it that did not mean love, and He tells us here immediately after it that the source of all the hard words He uses is love. His rebuking, His chastening, His threatening "as many as He loves." And He loves all. "As many as I love I rebuke and chasten! Be zealous, therefore, and repent."

I do not think that because you have passed through this and that experience, that therefore it is all right with you. The Christan life is a constant fighting. "What! are we to have no peace?" No; none till there is no sin left in you, till you are pure as Jesus Christ Himself. You are always crying out for peace, and you are as the workman that will go to sleep half the day and complain that he has not wages enough to live upon. What! you are getting to heaven cheap? You call it "getting into heaven." You think Jesus Christ came to save you from any suffering and to do you good. He came to save you from your sins, and until you are saved from them He will step between you and no suffering. "As many as I love I rebuke and chasten. Be zealous, therefore, and repent."

What Is Repentance?

What does "repent" mean? To weep that you have done something wrong? No; that is all very well, but that is not repentance. Is repentance to be vexed with yourself that you have fallen away from your own ideal, and you have done something as we all do every day that we ought to be ashamed of, because it is not up to the mark at all and we could have done better? No; that is not repentance. What is repentance? Turning your back upon the evil thing; pressing on to lay hold upon that for which Christ laid hold upon you. To repent is to think better of it, to turn away from the evil.

No man is ever condemned for the wicked things that he has done; he is condemned because he won't leave them. "This is the condemnation, that light is come into the world, and men love darkness rather than light because their deeds are evil." Full, free forgiveness—as free as God's blessed sunlight—to anybody who will just turn his back on the evil thing and go right; and if he will not—well, Christ is the Good Shepherd, but He keeps many terrible sheepdogs. If men will not turn from the evil way and come back to the fold, He sends out His monsters against them—for them, I should say, not "against them"; but with terror and shame, with pain and contempt, and loathing of themselves they will at last creep back, lame and haggard, to His fold. The longer you put it off the worse it will be for you, for you have got to come.

But now think how this fearful rebuke of the Lord ends in a promise. Well, if it were any but the Lord that said it—only no man would ever think to say it—it would not come into his mind; but if it came out of human mouth you would say: "How extravagant!" Look how the threat breaks off into an eternal glory of promise, and through the humblest figure of Himself He lifts us up by promise to the very throne of the Father. The Eternal Son of the Father speaks of Himself as a suppliant at our door. "Behold, I stand at the door and knock." "Knock!" Yes, you know it is a loving figure and you put it aside that way. You like pretty pictures of it; it is so sweet; and all the time He is knocking at your door and you do not let Him in. "I stand at the door and knock." It must have come from the Lord: there is no other heart it could have come from. John could not have invented it—he dare not; he was not big enough even to think it; it must have come from the Eternal Heart of Christ Himself. He speaks the things that satisfy me, and nothing else in heaven or earth ever did or ever can satisfy me.

At the Door Knocking

"Behold, I stand at the door and knock." Do you hear the knocking? "I do not want to make a fine speech to you—are you listening?" Do you hear Him knocking at your hearts? He wants to get in. What do I mean by that? Well, I mean this, that He wants to get to your inner house, your consciousness, your life, and to clean it out for you, and to turn out that self that you are always worshipping —to turn it out, and put the Eternal Father in its place, that you may be possessed no longer with

a false, foolish, contemptible idea of yourselves,
thinking yourselves noble and great and pure; for
that is what makes "self" contemptible, not when it
is humble, and listening, and thoughtful, and long-
ing, but when it feels all right—I say, He wants to
put the living God in your heart to possess it all. It
is His Father that He wants to see ruling there. He
is to be one with us in a way that there is no power
in our hearts to understand the closeness of it, no
figure in our language to say how close it is, for
unless you know how close the relation of Jesus
Christ to the Father you cannot know how close the
relation of every child of God, every creature that
He has made, is to his Father, his origin.

"If any man hear My voice." It is not the knocking, you see. He knocks to attract your attention,
and then you hear Him call, "Let Me in, let Me in!
Child, why will you not open the door? I am no
enemy; I am your own Companion, the thing you
have all the while been wanting, the lack of which
is the root of every misery in the world." When you
are unhappy, restless, dissatisfied, do not know
what to do with yourself, it is just because you have
not Christ in you as your friend. To know God by
knowing Christ, that is salvation, that is redemption, and nothing else is. Oneness with God is well-
being, it is not anything else.

"If any man hear My voice, and open the door, I
will come in to him, and will sup with him, and he
with Me." Filling the house with glory He will sit
down at your table a homely simple Guest.

When thou turnest away from evil,
Christ is this side of thy hill;
When thou turnest towards good,
Christ is walking in thy wood;
When thou sayest, "Father, pardon!"
Then the Lord is in thy garden;
When thou longest more and more,
Christ is knocking at the door;
When high hope thy songs doth rouse,
Then the Lord is in thy house;
But when love all else doth crown,
At thy table Christ sits down.

"If any man hear My voice and open the door, I will come in to him, and will sup with him, and he with Me." Do not you see there is no condescension in Jesus Christ? Such a thing is impossible. It is only a low nature thinking itself high that is capable of condescension. Jesus Christ comes to your level, knocks at your door. Ah! but if you will not open it to Him, He must get in somehow. To those that will not let Him in He may send a tempest that will blow the house to pieces, roof off, doors and windows off, that by the terror of death He may come in and cleanse it. But there is no condescension, and that is a thing that is most unlike all else that we see in the world.

But He goes beyond this; He not only says "I will come in to him, and will sup with him, and he with Me," but "To him that overcometh will I grant to sit with Me on My throne." Oh, never think that the figures of speech that the Lord uses mean less because they are figures! It will not satisfy Christ for any man but that he shall sit with Him on His throne. He is the one and the Eternal Man, and He will not be satisfied till all humanity—that is, every man and woman—sits on the throne of the glory that overcometh the world.

"Who, then, is He to reign over if they are all sitting on the throne with Him?" But that is your poor way of looking at the thing. The Lord does not want to reign that way. Does a father want to reign in his family by sitting in the high chair and looking down on his little ones? If he is a loving father he may have occasion to be a very severe one; but the end is that love shall rule in the hearts of all, and they shall be one family. So it is of Him of whom "all the families in heaven and earth are named." Why, the very notion of a family comes from the heart of God because He is the Father of all His creatures. He will rule just by loving, and the hearts of all will come to Him just because for very love they cannot help it. That is the rule of the kingdom of heaven, altogether the opposite of what we think of rule in this world. The man whom the world places highest is the man at the apex of the pyramid, and all the rest of the pyramid holds him up. The man who is highest in the notion of the heavenly kingdom is He—namely, Jesus Christ— who lies at the inverted apex of the pyramid. It is turned upside down for the kingdom of heaven. All rest on Him and all are built up on Him who has given Himself for us to deliver us from our sins.

Then He says: "To him that overcometh will I

grant to sit with Me on My throne, even as I also overcame, and am sat down with My Father on His throne." Then the Lord is not on one throne and ourselves upon another throne. "You must die with Me," He says—"die to all that is selfish and mean and low, and you must rise with Me into the love of God, and so you will sit on My Father's throne."

Oh, what a promise, far beyond what we can understand or know—far beyond! But are we, therefore, not to believe it, to believe something of it, to believe what we can lay hold of? And will you go tomorrow and give the whole strength of your nature to making money, putting business first; or will you go and give yourself to doing all you can to be happy—a false pursuit, for you cannot succeed; or will you believe what the Lord says: "Seek ye first the kingdom and righteousness of God and all things shall be added to you"?

We are such poor creatures that it is very hard to obey Jesus Christ. But He has offered to help you. God is doing what He can for every man; let Him have His way with you, and give yourself to Him heartily, with no reserve, and you will find that the troubles of the world shrink away, and, though the battle is hard, the strength grows!

8

Growth in Grace and Knowledge

> But grow in grace and in the knowledge of our
> Lord and Savior Jesus Christ.
>
> —II Peter 3:18

For a long time I did not care for the Epistles at all. They did not interest me at all. It was not that I had not read them or that I did not know something about them. But just because I did so, they were to me like a lumber room where all useless, broken, and old-fashioned things in the house which are not respected were put aside, heaped and gathered together.

Observe, I am not giving you my opinion about them at all, only my feeling. But I tell you that now they are to me precious beyond speech. And why? Because between the two experiences I have

learned to understand something of the Gospel. By
that I mean the story of the Lord Jesus Christ, His
good news, and, indeed, I foresaw that this would be
the consequence of knowing the Gospel.

Deliberately I put the Epistles aside, and said:
"When I know something of the Lord myself then,
and not till then, shall I understand what those
men meant who wrote about Him." When my heart
had something of that love which filled theirs, then,
and only then, could I hope to understand the great
utterances—for I believe they must be, though I
could not see it then—the great utterances of those
men.

Today I want you to look at one of these Epistles
with me.

The Second Epistle of Peter was the last of all to
be received as part of the Canon. There was much
difference of opinion about it. It is also perplexing to
find a great part of the Epistle of Jude almost word
for word with a large part of this Second Epistle of
Peter. I cannot understand it; I cannot explain it. I
have seen no theory to account for it. Doubtless
there is some very simple way.

But suppose that it is not Peter's at all; would
that have any effect upon the feeling with which I
regard it, perceiving in it the utterance of a strong
and true Christian soul? Not that I doubt it is
Peter's. It is like him, and I would like it all the
more to be certain it was his, because we know his
character, and it is a delightful thing to hear this
man talking about grace. I find in him—in his

Epistles—most wonderful signs of the power of this truth in Christ, to uplift, and purify, and strengthen the whole of an honest nature—yea, to cast out the falseness that clings to its honesty; for the most marvelous thing in our nature is, perhaps, that the good and bad may come so close together in the same man; and to hear Peter telling us to grow in grace, and in the knowledge of the Lord Jesus Christ, is precious, not merely because it is the best advice that can be given, but precious if we are able to believe that it comes from such a man as Peter. It has a power of its own, even different from the power it would have as coming from Paul, different from the power it would have as coming from John.

What Is Growth?

We must try to understand what he means, for words which do not move the heart and the soul are just to us everywhere what the Epistles were to me until I understood something of the heart of those that wrote them. First of all, I need not so much try to explain growing as to enforce it. What would you say is the main and prominent difference between what we call the mineral kingdom and the vegetable and the animal? As near as we can say the one grows and the other does not; therefore, we speak of life in the one and of the lack of life in the other. I am not sure myself at all that there is not a lower kind of life even in the vegetable; but there is this

difference—that these conditions that we call life
in the animal come from the inside, and that in the
case of the vegetable the growth is by the attraction
of homogeneous particles. The lower growth is by
accretion, that of growing to the outside, layer upon
layer; whereas in the higher, in what we call life, it
all comes from the inside. It is an unseen power
within that causes the gathering together of matter
from without. And when we come up to the higher
world, the mental, the spiritual world, the same
thing holds in higher kinds and in wonderful ways.
If I say to a Christian man: "Are you growing?"
what do I mean? The meaning is not far to seek,
surely. I have a right to ask him if he grows, when
we are told that we are branches of that vine of
which the Master is the root and the stem. So the
Master speaks of Himself as the head and we as
members of His body.

We are told by the Apostle Paul that every person must grow in the fullness of Christ. But, as I
said myself, my object is not so much to explain as
to enforce. I have no great interest in mere instruction; it would not move me to send me up into the
pulpit if I could not rouse to life, if I could not, in
any way, enforce the eternal fact of God and man.
That is something for which a man ought to be willing to die. But the mere instruction of what is, or is
not, the education of the brain, the mind, does not
interest me enough. And in this age in which there
is as much idolatry of intellect as there is of money
—and the one is as much idolatry as the other—I,

for my part, protest that rather than be a king of science I would be an idiot with a heart. It is better to love a little than to know everything; and, more than that, the man that loves alone shall be the man that knows. There is nothing yet worthy of the name of science. We are but feeling our way, and the man that loves well, when the true time comes, will outstrip all the searchers in the knowledge of the very things that the intellect desires to understand.

Are you growing? In what direction are you growing? You cannot stand still. If you have been settling down upon a general well-meaningness of mind and heart; if you are reposing after what, perhaps, you would think labors that have earned rest; if you are free from strong temptations to anything that is very wicked, it is possible that in the gathering weariness of years, and in the fact that up to this time, perhaps, you have been directing your main efforts toward ease of body and mind in declining years, by gaining the means to live without labor— it is possible that you may have just sunk, as it were, into the easy chair of indifference, and that the life has now ceased to send forth fresh roots for growth. To compare you to a tree, I may say the nakedness is creeping down the branches and the boughs, and that you are dying before you die.

If you consider the matter at all, do you think: "Well, I shall get on somehow or other in the new life that is coming"? But you would, if you had your way, just go on not troubling anybody, nor hoping to be troubled. Oh, if we are not growing upward we are growing downward! A man may get into a worse condition by stupidity and indifference than a man may even now be in who has broken some of the main commandments.

Do you love God more than you did? Does your heart swell to think that God is? Is it to you the crowning bliss—God! just as He is? Do you delight in pondering on the words of the Lord? Do you go forth to turn them into actions? Knowledge without action, even though it may put on the lovely name of faith, is but a foreign thing in the human soul. It is not the true genuine thing; and it causes sores and festerings. Do you care about Jesus Christ? Do you think of Him as One who lived two thousand years ago, or as One who is now in the world, and is the same now as He was then, and had been from all eternity? Do you think He left the world? No; He only vanished that He might come nearer, and after some little time He kept appearing to the disciples when they least expected Him. He could appear in any moment, for He was there. Is the story of Christ to you the greatest truth; or is it a tradition, after which it is the custom of decent people to accommodate themselves to certain ways of life? Either we are one with Christ in some vital, growing way, be it ever so little, or we are not with Him, and we have no life in us. I speak as one who is beginning to wake up from the dead, and I cry to you: "Awake, thou that sleepest, and arise from the dead, and Christ will give thee light."

Converted Every Day

The constant tendency is to go to sleep, and there are many, I suspect, that think that because they have gone through a certain experience, which they call conversion, they are all right. We need to be converted every day. I need to be turned toward the eternal way from the passing, from the phenomenal—yea, and turned from myself more than all up toward the Life and the Source of my being. Do you think that this life is for its own self or for the sake of the deeper life—that life which is one with God, thinking His thoughts, rejoicing in His joy, judging with His judgments? That is life; it is for the sake of that that this life is. We are sent here that we may know Jesus Christ and grow thereby, not know about Him. To know about Him is not enough. We must know the Man Himself—His thoughts, His feelings, His intents, His conditions of being. We must understand them, and become one with them.

Do not be content not to grow. If you are not growing bigger you are growing less. If the light is not increasing, the darkness is encroaching. Let me try you with one very plain little test. When did you do anything because Jesus Christ said we must do so?

Ask yourselves, when did you do any single thing, because that Man, the Eternal Son of the living God, moving your very hearts toward it, impelled you to do it? If you cannot think of anything that He says, that is a bad sign. You have not been trying to obey Him, or you would think of many things that He says. Instead, you would be feeling now that He is requiring more and more and more of you, and as you go on in life you would be more aware of the difficulty of the effort, and strain to work out your own salvation—yea, you would be in despair if you did not believe that it was God that was working in you. It is no light thing to set out to pass from the kingdom of salvation into the kingdom of God, to pass from the world of outside things with sensual appeal to the eternal, changeless, blessed religion of life and peace and obedience.

I say: Have you obeyed the law of Christ once within the last year? Have you done anything today, or yesterday, or last month, just because the Lord said so; or have you been trying to turn aside and explain away and make light of the great demands that He makes upon you, in which greatness lies your liberty and deliverance?

There is in the heart of all of us a power that works for the commonplace, and which, instead of accepting the grand things of Christ, says that is impossible; and then, when the voice would not say it and the heart would hardly bear to think it, the conscience permits the will to disregard it, and that is worse than all. Did Christ mean you were to love your enemies? Do you try to love your enemies? It is said that you cannot serve God and mammon; and yet, though He says: "Therefore, take no thought for the morrow," you begin to argue that you must.

You are not Christians. How can you be if this is your tone toward Him? The Lord is very easy to please. He will be pleased with the smallest growth; but He is very hard to satisfy. He will never be satisfied until you are one with Him in perfect purity and strength. Wake up, and what is left us in our life let us give heartily, intensely, and obediently unto Him.

We are to grow, the Apostle here says, increase in the knowledge of our Savior Jesus Christ. I prefer to think, from the Greek, that it means grow in *the* grace and in the knowledge of the Lord Jesus Christ. If you put the *the* to the one, you had better put it to the other: "Grow in *the* grace of Jesus Christ." Is it not a fact that although you have been used to hearing the word "grace," yet you have a very vague idea, indeed, of what it means? You think it is something that belongs to the Bible and the Church and heaven, and all that. What is grace? The root of the word is a verb that means "I rejoice, I am glad." Grace is anything to make the heart glad with pure gladness; the grace of God, the grace of Jesus is the graciousness, the gentleness, the harmony of life in God and in His Son. You speak to a graceful person—you cannot define it; but it makes a kind of something which is more than satisfaction—it is pleasure, it is the recognition of a spiritual thing even when you see it in the human form, yet more when you see the graciousness of one man or one woman toward another. That is the harmony between the being of the one and the being of the other—the recognition by the one of the same nature, and the same needs, and the same readiness to be met, to be pleased, or to be hurt, to be sorrowful or glad, as in the person himself; the submission of the one nature to the demands of another nature—that is grace, that is graciousness. This, of course, is the root that works out all form, and all that is not rooted in this will pass away and wither, and where this inward grace, the true relation between the one and the other exists, it will cast off all outside discord, all ugliness of form, and will put on its own robes of beauty.

The Graciousness of Jesus

Just let me give you an instance or two of the grace of our Lord Jesus Christ. When the leper came to Him crying for a remedy He spoke, and we know that His word was enough; but that would not satisfy the graciousness of the Lord Jesus Christ. He would not give the man his cure as He might have given him an alms, or, rather, I should say, as if He had thrown him an alms. The poor man was terribly cut off from his people, looked upon as defiled, and so horrid that nobody would touch him. It is a terrible thing to show disgust at any human being; but these lepers were used to expressions of disgust from their fellow men. There came the graciousness of our Lord Jesus Christ, the grace of Christ, for He must put His hands upon him, saying: "I will, be thou clean." That was not necessary

for the leper's sake, but the grace was needful for
the poor man's soul and spirit. This is the grace of
our Lord Jesus Christ.

I will tell you another instance. The Lord was
once at a marriage feast, and they had no wine.
They had run out of it, and He made more. That
was gracious; but that is not what I am going to
speak about at present. He did it, but He did not go
there intending to do it; He did not want to do it. It
was at the entreaty of His mother, and to please His
mother that He did it; of course, if it had been
wrong He would not have done it to please His
mother or anybody else. His time was not come—
He did not mean to begin it; but as she wanted it He
could afford to do it, and He did it, and there is the
grace of our Lord Jesus Christ.

Yes; and some of His hardest words are full of
graciousness. Sometimes, for the sake of others, He
inflicted pain even upon those to whom He spoke;
but, oh! how He yielded afterward: "It is not meet to
take the children's bread, and to cast it to the dogs."
But we do not see how He looked when He said it.
That was the lesson to His disciples. They had all
more or less of the Pharisee in them at the time:
"That is the way you think of those that are not of
your nation." He put their thoughts into words, and
spoke them to the woman, and then afterward re-
buked them by saying: "How great was her faith!"
and, even more graciously: "Oh, woman, great is
thy faith; be it unto thee as thou wilt!" There was

the graciousness of our Lord Jesus Christ just coming out of seeming hardness.

And you remember at the last, when looking down from the cross He saw two whom He loved best on earth—His mother and His friend John—He could not say much, but He must make them one by the holiest bond, and while He was going away to be more of a sovereign than ever, yet should there be a new motherhood, a new sonship: "Woman, behold thy son"; "Son, behold thy mother." That is a kind of legacy the Lord leaves behind Him. "Love one another"; He left us love for His legacy. He cared that the hearts He was loving should grow in personal affection for each other—genuine love, mother love, son love. There is the graciousness of our Lord Jesus Christ.

Are we growing in that? Do you ever put away a troubled look off your face because you know it will give trouble to your family? Do you scowl at home, or is your entrance to your own people as new breaking light to their day? Are they glad when you go out of the house, or does a little blank fall upon them till you return? What are you? Are you gracious? Have you anything of the grace of the Lord Jesus Christ? Do you cultivate it? Are you vexed with yourselves when you have lost your temper? And do you try hard to overcome that evil thing that occasions more unhappiness in this world, perhaps, than anything else? Oh, what a pity it is that we men should so often cause unhappiness to the women about us! Oh, to be gentle, genial, strong, merry! Oh, to be gracious! Are you courteous to those that come nearest you, and brother-loving, cheerful? If men would love each other yet better, they would be courteous; for there is a genuine courtesy that is not dependent at all upon the mere outside forms. There is a tone of words. Why speak roughly, indifferently, if your heart is not rough and indifferent? There is a strong geniality in the grace of Christ, the graciousness of God, that ought to be cultivated between the nearest friends, and, most of all, between husband and wife. Are you growing in the grace of Christ? If you are not getting more pleasant, I doubt if you are growing in anything.

But then comes this strange word, the *knowledge* of Jesus Christ. Now, I know that if we do not know what Jesus Christ is we have not eternal life. To know God through Christ by knowing the heart of Christ, to know the heart of God, that is to have eternal life, to be one with God by knowing Him with your whole being, so that you have no will that can move one hair's breadth against His will.

I suggest this interpretation as a help. We are to grow in the graciousness and in the knowledge of Jesus Christ. We are to become gracious like Him; we are to grow in the knowledge of Jesus Christ. I put that as a means always to grow in the knowledge that Jesus Christ had. We are to grow in His knowledge. What did He know? What do we know? We have been growing by our own kinds of knowledge from the very moment that our eyes opened upon the world, and I trust some have also been growing in Christ's knowledge.

What does Christ know? Well, first of all, and it is the root of all His joy and existence, He knows God. Jesus Christ knows God, and you see He is perfectly, absolutely satisfied with God. Doubts come up in our hearts about God and His dealings with us, and we look to the story of Jesus, and we see He was just like us in that He suffered and toiled; and when we see that He was perfect, and entirely, utterly satisfied with His Father, as being perfection itself, may we not, then, take comfort to our hearts and fall before Him, and say, with Job: "Though He slay me, yet will I trust Him," for the Master knew Him. That was the beginning and root of the knowledge of Jesus. He knew His Father, and was everlastingly content with Him.

Then Jesus Christ knew men. We do not try enough to know our fellow men. We are ready enough to judge them; but we do not try enough to understand them—to know what they are, to see what it is at the root that makes them do this or that. We should give ourselves an opportunity to understand humanity, to know those who are about us, and from them to know the individual, until we are a hiding place from the wind, a covert from the tempest, as the shadow of a great rock in a weary land. Every Christian ought to be a refuge. I believe that, if we were like Christ, even the wild beasts of our woods and fields would flee to us for refuge and deliverance; and man must be in the world as He was in the world, and then the world will blossom around him with all God's meanings, and not merely with men's sayings.

We shall grow in the graciousness and in the knowledge of the Lord Christ until we ourselves are blessed with the same joy with which Christ was blessed, until we are glad with the eternal gladness of the eternal God.

9

Eternal Harmony

PREACHED AT TRINITY CONGREGATIONAL CHURCH, GLASGOW

At that time Jesus answered and said, "I thank Thee, O Father, Lord of heaven and earth, because Thou hast hid these things from the wise and prudent and hast revealed them unto babes. Even so, Father: for it seemed good in Thy sight. All things are delivered unto Me of My Father: and no man knoweth the Son, but the Father; neither knoweth any man the Father, save the Son, and He to whomsoever the Son will reveal Him. Come unto Me all ye that labor and are heavy laden, and I will give you rest. Take My yoke upon you, and learn of Me; for I am meek and lowly in heart; and ye shall find rest unto your souls. For My yoke is easy and My burden is light."

—Matthew 11:25–30

This passage in Matthew has always delighted me. It seems like a link between Matthew and the Gospel of John.

You know, there is a great deal of unlikeness between the first three Gospels, which we call the Synoptic Gospels, and the fourth, which is John's Gospel. There is no contradiction in them whatever and their unlikeness is no difficulty to me.

But this passage is like a rivet passing between the others and the Gospel of John. In fact, it is like reading a piece of John itself.

Whether it was that the Lord said many things to John that He did not say to the others, or that these reporters, of whom Matthew was the only one that knew Him, were not capable of taking up many of the things that John was capable of understanding, I need not stop to inquire.

We know that John came nearest to the Lord, and we have more of the Lord's mind and will in John's Gospel than anywhere else. But here Matthew has got a hold of a precious passage, part of which John himself did not have.

What I want you to note chiefly is how the call of our Lord, "Come unto Me," is founded on what goes before. The spiritual logic of the passage runs through all that I have read. I need not stop now to speak about why the Lord thanked the Father that He had revealed these things to the fishermen about Him, and to the women about Him, and not to the wise and prudent; it was simply that the wise and prudent would have spoiled it all—those that were knowing and learned, and wanted to get things all put into shape according to their philosophy and their modes of thinking—they have done terrible damage in the Church of Christ. The simple heart that begins by obedience comes to know verily the will of the Master. He that gives his energy to expounding God, instead of obeying Him, has been a curse to his fellows. No man can understand God but he who gives the energy of his being to do the will of the Master.

Christ declares in connection with this: "No man can know the Father but he that understands the Son"—who knoweth the Son. He says what amounts to this: "You do not know Me; the Father knows Me. You do not know the Father except as I tell you of the Father; except as you come to know Me you cannot know the Father." All the metaphysics in the world may be true, but all that they can tell you is *about* God, is *about* Him, but they don't *give* you God; you cannot get God that way. You must know Jesus Christ as a man knows his friend. You must know Him as you know the dearest man or woman in the world, only much better, infinitely more, or you know nothing about God—rather, I should say, you may know many things about God, but you do not know God; and you have not eternal life, for that is the knowledge of God, and nothing else—nothing else. Having laid this down that He knows the Father, He has asserted, "I know the Father." Just think for a moment who says it. Even men who do not give themselves up to Him will acknowledge that, at least, He was the best of men, that multitudes acknowledge a great deal more who do not give themselves to Him at all. Perhaps they think to flatter Him by consenting to this or that theory about Him, but they do not give themselves to Him. I say, however, that all who know anything about Him agree that, at least, He was the best of men. Then, what follows? Either this best of men stated, made very solemn high statements concerning God which were all false (and note the contradiction—the best of men telling the most presumptuous lies), or else Jesus Christ did know God, and spake out of the depths of an infinite and eternal knowledge of God. And upon this He found His call, "Come unto Me," "I know the Father." He says, "The Father knows Me; knows I am speaking the truth; I know the Father: come unto Me, and I will give you rest."

Sure am I that it will never be well with us until we know the Father. And Jesus Christ knows the Father in the same way. We cannot know Him with that splendid perfection with which the Eternal Son knows the Eternal Father, but we must know Him after the same fashion—for these hearts of ours will never be at peace. Jesus says, "I know the Father," and it is in the strength of this knowledge that He comes to you and me and all of us, and says, "Come unto Me." The business of the Lord Jesus is to lead us, the little ones, His little brothers and sisters, home to the eternal home, where the essence of all home-feeling is just the very air of it—

home to the Father's knees, to the Father's arms—
nay, nay, to His very heart, to His very soul, where
all is well, gloriously well. Life is something worth
living then, never will be till then, and is worth
living now only in the prospect of this eternal harmony between the Father and His children.

But let us see how this is to work. He says,
"Come unto Me, and I will give you rest." The rest
of Jesus Christ was just in His Father. The very
delight of Jesus Christ was in His Father. The
whole world hangs on the fact that Jesus was just
full, in the eternity of His Being, with love to, and
delight in, His Father; that is the strength and the
joy of the Son of God. And, knowing His Father, He
comes and calls the rest of His children: "Come unto
Me."

Thanking God for Trouble

But, of course, those only will come that are
somehow troubled. If we had a little clearer insight
into things, a man would go down on his knees the
moment a trouble comes to him to thank God for it;
and I am not speaking extravagantly. Ah! which of
us is equal to that? Only those that know something
about trouble, some kind or other, are waked up to
hear the calling voice of the Lord: "Come unto Me,
all ye that labor and are heavy laden."

But is there anybody that has no trouble? I have
not known anybody yet. Oh! do not let anybody say

to you it is only when you are in trouble for *your sins* that you can come to Him. That is not what is meant at all. Why, if you are in trouble about your sins, you are very near the help. It is the man that is in *any* trouble, as I said already. But the Lord speaks here to everybody that has anything to make them uncomfortable, not at rest, who has anything in heart or mind that just worries them; no matter what it is; it is a thing that God does not want in you. Why, finally, the end of God is that we shall be all at perfect peace, and in the triumph of strength. Whoever has trouble is away from God; and the good of it is this, that when the trouble comes it lets us know that we are not with God. I believe myself that every discontent in the human heart is just a crying out for God, though the heart does not know it. The cause may be a very poor thing; it may be mean of us to be troubled about the thing that does trouble us sometimes; but no matter, it is the cry of the divine nature in us. For the devil did not make us. We come out of the heart of God.

And I say that every trouble is the cry of the divine life in us, which we have wronged, as we have wronged God, the Father. I do not say the man knows it; that is another thing; for did he know it, he would be near home; and he is a long way off.

Promises come to us like the little birds about us that we want to catch. They fly away beyond to a branch, and when the child goes after the bird, the bird flies further and further, and so the enticing birds of God will never rest till they have taken us home. What is the good of hope if we hope in the wrong thing? Ah! even the sorrow that follows is a help in its way. But a new hope comes and flies before us.

Oh! do not say that hope is delusive. You may have chosen the wrong hope to follow, but it is God Himself who is the Father of hope in our hearts. And for my part I have never had so much hope as I have now, and it grows and grows till it is infinite. And even your troubles, be they disappointed hopes, or be they what they may—whether they be the sacred troubles of loss of friends by death, or the unholy troubles—unholy troubles, I mean, in their cause, that come from falseness, wrongness in those about you, or wrongness in yourself—all these troubles are just things to drive you to the Master who is calling you.

The Sheep and the Sheepdogs

When I think of the Lord as a Shepherd, I see the love of His sheep in His face and in His eyes, gracious and tender and self-forgetting. But He has a terrible set of sheepdogs round Him, and they have fearful names. There is Pain, and Fear, and Anxiety, and Shame. Oh! there are many of them; they follow at His heel; but if there is a strayed sheep away on the hill that won't turn at the call of the Master, He speaks a word to one of His dogs, and away speeds that dog after the sheep that won't turn. Oh! they are sacred creatures those dogs, too, for they work the will of the Father.

We must be made clean, and if we do not come to Him to be made clean, His dogs come after us. All the trouble you are in, you may call just the Shepherd's dogs that come to fetch you back to the fold, the fold which is the vestibule to the kingdom of heaven, the right knowledge of Christ.

You must get into the fold if you want to have an idea of Jesus Christ. There is not a selfish thought in Him. He will give His very soul, His life for you, but if suffering is needful to make you meet it you must, for He is not going to treat us like animals, compelling us without our will to do this or do that. The glory of God is this, that He demands us to take a share with Him in our own creation; for I say we are not created yet, we are only in process of creation in the image of God, and He demands that we shall take a share in it. We must will the will of God, and so He sends His troubles to wake us up, and to make us choose to be on His side against ourselves. And for this purpose is the whole constitution of the world as it is. It grows clearer and plainer to me as I live longer that this is His way in working people, and going through history I see that the whole thing is made ever a means of compelling us who have come out from God to make our circle back to the bosom of the Father. And here the Lord is calling: "Come unto Me all ye that labor and are heavy laden." If we are afraid of the Shepherd's dogs, there is no refuge but with the Shepherd Himself. If you are frightened at them, away back to the Shepherd, and the dogs will be your servants. The right path is the safe path. He will give you rest.

He says, "Come unto Me; I will give you rest." But how? Not that we have the right to ask how, to begin with. What we have got to do is to go to Him. Do not wait till you understand, but go to Him. This is not hard to do. A child runs to his mother when he is in any trouble. If you are in any trouble run to the Lord. You do not see Him. No; but surely He has given you imagination enough to make you capable of believing that He will hear you when you speak. It is the thought of God that makes me think, and if God did not think, I could not think, and so what is more reasonable than that I should be with God, of the same mind with God, taking what He tells me as the merest, simplest of things. Why should I ask to understand Him before I do what He tells me? If this Man says unto me "Come to Me," I come to Him. I cannot see Him, but He must hear me, else the whole thing is a confusion, a chaos, a falsehood, and the sooner we cease to exist the better.

But here He does tell us how it is: "Come unto Me, and I will give you rest"; "Take My yoke upon you"—that is the way—"and learn of Me." Now, what does this "yoke" mean? Many people have the idea that the Lord takes a yoke and lays it upon you, and that He says, as it were holding the yoke in His hand: "Come here, and take My yoke upon you." That is not it at all.

"My yoke" means the yoke that I bear, not the yoke that I lay upon you, but the yoke that I am bearing. The Eternal Son of God tells us that His own rest of soul, His own peace of mind, just comes from the yoke that He Himself bears. We do not often see in this country two oxen yoked together: but where I live you see not unfrequently two lovely oxen walking together with one yoke across the necks of both. That is the idea here. It does not even mean "Take a yoke upon you like that yoke which I am wearing." I have said already it does not mean "Take the yoke that I have got to lay upon you," neither does it mean "Take a yoke upon you like the yoke I am wearing." But it means "Take the other end of My yoke and walk with Me, harnessed with Me; we will go together and draw the burden of the Father's will." I remember a little pictorial passage in the "Purgatory," where Dante is walking along with one of the burdened souls, where pride— which makes one walk erect and strut—is punished with a heavy burden on the back, to wit, the burden of their own pride. And Dante is talking to one of these men, and because the man cannot stand up, Dante stoops down to get his mouth and his ear near to the mouth and the ear of the man he is talking to and he says: "So we went along together like two oxen in one yoke."

Now that is just the picture of the union that is in the mind of Jesus when He is speaking about the yoke here: "Be yoke-fellow with Me; take one end of the yoke." The burden is the Father's will. "Take My yoke upon you, and learn of Me, for I am meek and lowly in heart." When that ugly thing rises up in us—pride, resentment, thinking about self, that inclination to assert our individual self as against somebody else—oh! remember the Lord Christ then. Be ready to be slain, as the Lord was slain, rather than that. It is not cowardice I am pleading for. I am pleading against the worship of self. Lord Christ, make us meek and lowly in heart, for that is the only dignity, the only nobility.

"And ye shall find rest to your souls," He says. Do you believe it would put you to rest if you gave yourself up heart, soul, brain, body, to the Lord Christ to do His will? Well, you cannot be sure of it, till you try it, perhaps. But at least you may believe the Lord Christ enough to try what He tells you: "Take My yoke upon you and ye shall find rest to your souls." Now, that is what we want.

The Pursuit of Happiness

Some people spend their lives pursuing happiness. Poor creatures! As if they could make themselves happy by getting hold of things that are inferior to themselves. If you want peace you must get hold of what is greater than yourself, namely, of God Himself. We have nothing to do with hunting after happiness, that is not our business. Seek ye first the kingdom and righteousness of God, and the rest will be added to you. The Father will see that His children are happy. It won't be the Father's fault, if the children will only mind their own business; that is what He tells them. If we do the thing that the Master says, you will find your troubles begin to be bearable, and by and by you will find they are not such bad things at all, and then will such an opening appear amongst the clouds about you that you will be able to believe in the possibility of a condition of perfect rest and quiet, and to feel that it is coming.

Just as your will takes the will of God for its sole guide, so do you begin to be quiet, or, simply, you begin to be good children. That is it. As soon as the child gives up what is forbidden him and begins to try to do what his father and mother tell him, the child is quiet, at peace—the highest simile we have of the high relation in which we stand to God. It is so simple that only a person with a child's heart can see how essentially, eternally, and absolutely true it is. But the plague of it is that so many are bent on sin that they never set themselves to obey, and, of course, they are miserably sad. We must take the yoke of God's will upon us, and then we shall find rest to our souls. Some people hunger for death even for the sake of rest. That is not the way to get it. Of course, it is more life we want to put us at rest, and this is the way to get the life eternal—to know God.

And then, just note the last words here: "Ye shall find rest unto your souls, for My yoke is easy and my burden is light." Does He mean to say to you: "You need not mind it; it is not very heavy"? No; that is not what He means. He means: "The yoke that I am bearing is easy; the burden I have to draw is light. Come and try My yoke. Come and help Me to draw My burden. Let the will of the Father be your burden, as it is Mine, and the yoke to you be that you are His obedient child as I am. For My yoke, I find, is easy: My burden, I find, is light."

Remember that He said this when the vision of the cross was not far ahead on the road in which He was drawing the will of God along. Think of that, that He saw the cross at the end! We have got used to the sight and the thought of the cross! Never was death to a criminal so terrible or more terrible than that execrated load and detested punishment. Think what it was! But if you and I are not prepared, rather than do the thing that is against the will of God, to be nailed to the cross, even as Jesus Christ was, with nails through our hands and our feet, we are not worthy of Him; we are not Christians in the high, true, deep, real sense. It was a terrible thing to hang there enduring that torture that brought sickness and death. And the Lord saw it. This is what I want to dwell upon, not the terrors, but the fact that the Lord, seeing these things before Him, yet said, "My yoke is easy...My burden is light."

Then remember what made Him say so—just the knowledge of His Father. He had such a Father that for Him He would bear anything. He is the same to the end—a thing intelligible to every human heart. The Lord loved the Father so (He knew Him to be so good, so perfect), without one atom of self-glorification or selfishness, and was utterly devoted to Him and to all His creatures. Jesus was so content with His Father, so full of bliss because His Father was just what He was, that for His sake He says, "My yoke is easy . . . My burden is light."

Oh! shall we be such poor miserable creatures as to say that our yoke is heavy, that the burden is not light? If it be so, it is because we do not know God enough. For the Lord Christ knew the Father so well that the utmost horror that this world could lay upon Him was to Him easy and light. You do not suppose He would not feel it, that He would not be allowed to suffer. God forbid that such a thought should dwell in our minds one moment. It was not the lessening of the pain, but the exceeding glory of Him for whose sake He bore it; and Whose glory was present in His heart, and mind, and whole Being, making Him able to carry the yoke, able to draw the burden.

ABOUT THE AUTHOR

George MacDonald (1824 – 1905), a Scottish preacher and poet, was one of the most influential and original writers of Victorian literature. His unorthodox theology alarmed his congregation and prompted his resignation from Trinity Congregational Church, but he continued to preach as an itinerant lecturer. Though dogmatic Calvinists opposed him, MacDonald won an enormous audience with his nearly thirty novels, aimed at broadening religious ideals. But his enduring reputation rests on his fairy tales, the best of which are regarded as children's classics, such as *The Princess and the Goblin*. His contemporaries considered him far more original than his friend Lewis Carroll. His most significant adult fantasies, *Phantastes* and *Lilith*, illustrate his conception of resurrection. The works of C.S. Lewis, W.H. Auden and G.K. Chesterton attest to the power of MacDonald's imagination, which continues to entertain and inspire today.